BBC

DOCTOR WHO

THE COMPLETE HISTORY

DOCTOR WHO
THE COMPLETE HISTORY

How to continue your collection

Subscribe online at **www.dwcompletehistory.com**
or call **0333 300 1510**.
From ROI call **0333 300 1511**.
(Calls from a landline are charged at your local rate)

CUSTOMER SERVICE, SUBSCRIPTIONS & BACK ORDERS IN OVERSEAS MARKETS
AUSTRALIA: Visit www.bissettmags.com.au or call (03) 9872 4000
NEW ZEALAND: Ask your local magazine retailer or write to: Netlink, PO Box 47906, Ponsonby, Auckland.

EDITOR JOHN AINSWORTH
DOCTOR WHO MAGAZINE EDITOR TOM SPILSBURY
ART EDITOR RICHARD ATKINSON
DESIGNER PAUL VYSE
COVER AND STORY MONTAGES LEE JOHNSON
PRODUCTION ASSISTANTS PETER WARE, MARK WRIGHT
ORIGINAL PRODUCTION NOTES ANDREW PIXLEY
ADDITIONAL MATERIAL JONATHAN MORRIS, RICHARD ATKINSON,
ALISTAIR McGOWN
WITH THANKS TO ANN BARRETT, JAMES DUDLEY, NIC HUBBARD,
BRIAN MINCHIN, STEVEN MOFFAT, KIRSTY MULLEN, MATT NICHOLLS,
MARTIN ROSS, EDWARD RUSSELL, BBC WALES, BBC WORLDWIDE
AND BBC.CO.UK

MANAGING DIRECTOR MIKE RIDDELL
MANAGING EDITOR ALAN O'KEEFE

BBC Worldwide, UK Publishing:
DIRECTOR OF EDITORIAL GOVERNANCE NICHOLAS BRETT
DIRECTOR OF CONSUMER PRODUCTS AND PUBLISHING
ANDREW MOULTRIE
HEAD OF UK PUBLISHING CHRIS KERWIN
PUBLISHER MANDY THWAITES
PUBLISHING CO-ORDINATOR EVA ABRAMIK
UK.Publishing@bbc.com
www.bbcworldwide.com/uk--anz/ukpublishing.aspx

Partwork Authority,
Marketing and Distribution:
Hachette Partworks Ltd
Jordan House
47 Brunswick Place
London N1 6EB
www.hachettepartworks.com

MANAGING EDITOR (HACHETTE) SARAH GALE
PUBLISHER (HACHETTE) HELEN NALLY

Distributed in the UK and Republic of Ireland
by Hachette Partworks Ltd & Marketforce.

Printed in Spain   ISSN 2057-6048   ALL RIGHTS RESERVED

© 2015 Panini UK Ltd

Contents

Welcome

New York, New York – so good that they visited it twice. Yes, that's right! New York is the setting for two of the four stories, starring David Tennant as the Tenth Doctor, featured in this volume. In truth though, the New York of *Gridlock* – 'New' New York – is a completely different city, on a completely different world to the more familiar 'Big Apple' of *Daleks in Manhattan/Evolution of the Daleks*. The two cities, and the two stories themselves, couldn't be further apart. In fact, all four stories in this volume superbly demonstrate the breadth and variety of settings, time periods, and types of story that *Doctor Who* encompasses: from a bleak far future in *Gridlock*, to Dalek plots during America's Great Depression of the 1930s in *Daleks in Manhattan/Evolution of the Daleks*, to genetic tampering in present day London in *The Lazarus Experiment*, and back to the future onboard a doomed spaceship, plummeting into a sun, in *42*. Each story is a self-contained mini-movie. It's hard to imagine that anyone could ever get bored with *Doctor Who*.

Of course, although each of the four stories is self-contained and can be enjoyed in its own right, there are some ongoing story threads running through them. Not least of these is the evolution of Martha Jones from tag-along traveller to fully fledged Companion. It has to be said that the Doctor is a little bit reluctant to embrace Martha as his new shipmate – he's still smarting from his recent forced separation from Rose Tyler [see *Army of Ghosts/Doomsday* – Volume 53] and isn't in a hurry to get close to anyone new. But Martha's having none of it, and puts the Doctor on the spot at the end of *Gridlock*, forcing him to open up and reveal the details of his past. And then again, at the end of *The Lazarus Experiment*, Martha initially declines another trip in the TARDIS, feeling the Doctor is just giving her a series of one-off "treats". The Doctor relents and acknowledges Martha's true status as a travelling companion, rather than just a passenger. He even presents her with her very own TARDIS key at the end of *42*.

We also see some foreshadowing of dark events in the future. With his dying words, the ancient Face of Boe tells the Doctor in *Gridlock* that he is not alone... while on present day Earth, election fever is in the air with the unseen Mr Saxon tipped to be the next prime minister. But why is Mr Saxon so interested in Martha Jones, warning her mother that the Doctor is a dangerous man? All will be revealed in the climactic final three episodes of the 2007 series – *Utopia/The Sound of Drums/Last of the Time Lords* [2007 – see Volume 56].

John Ainsworth – Editor

Right:
Humanity grinds to a halt in the distant future.

'THE DOCTOR ACKNOWLEDGES MARTHA'S TRUE STATUS AS A TRAVELLING COMPANION, RATHER THAN JUST A PASSENGER.'

GRIDLOCK

> STORY 181

The Doctor and Martha arrive on New Earth in the far future. New New York is deserted, with the remains of the population trapped on a subterranean motorway, unaware of the fate that awaits them at their final destination.

Introduction

Nine years on from the Eighth Doctor TV Movie [1996 – see Volume 47], 16 years on from the end of the last full series, new executive producer Russell T Davies was presented with a challenge: how do you illustrate the series' broad scope to new viewers? This is perhaps why each of his series begins with one episode rooted in the present, has another drawn from the the pages of history and sets one in the far-flung future.

To emphasise its point, this escapade takes us further into the future than ever before. A dizzying thought that had been used to great effect in stories like *The Ark* [1966 – see Volume 7] and *Frontios* [1984 – see Volume 38] which, like *Gridlock*, examine how humanity, with all its strengths and weaknesses, persists. In this instance, it's leading up to the conclusion of the 2007 series, which takes the idea to its ultimate extreme – imagining the final throes of a dying universe, at the point where all life ceases to exist.

The third part of a loose trilogy featuring the Face of Boe, *Gridlock* sees our annual return to the year five billion, previously visited in 2005 and 2006's establishing futuristic forays *The End of the World* [see Volume 48] and *New Earth* [see Volume 51]. In addition to re-establishing the core principles on which the series is based, Davies also implemented his own approach, and such linking strands between episodes and across series were not uncommon.

As early as his second year in charge, Davies felt his version of the series was popular enough to indulge in arguably obscure references to old *Doctor Who*. Here, he resurrected the parasitic entity behind 1967's *The Macra Terror* [see Volume 10] – crab-like monsters had been brought to life as best as they could be back in the 60s, were now digitally rendered in all their scuttling, pincer-snapping glory.

The cryptic prophecies of Boe or the threat of the Macra, however, are not the focus of this story. It's mainly about a community of people stranded on a futuristic motorway; civilisation hangs by a thread, but in the end humanity will always unite to overcome adversity. The story also deals with the delicate topic of drugs, considers notions of redemption, and cements the relationship between the Doctor and his new companion, Martha Jones.

Gridlock is certainly a good example of how *Doctor Who* is sometimes set in the future, but it's also so much more. ∎

Below:
The Doctor and Martha take a peek at what's above them.

'GRIDLOCK IS LEADING UP TO THE CONCLUSION OF THE 2007 SERIES, WHICH IMAGINES A DYING UNIVERSE WHERE ALL LIFE CEASES TO EXIST.'

STORY

An 'American Gothic' couple radio for help from their fogbound car. Something is trying to get in! [1]

The Doctor offers to take Martha on one more trip. She suggests they visit his home planet. The Doctor describes it – "the sky's a burnt orange, with the Citadel enclosed in a mighty glass dome" – but suggests they go to New New York instead.

They land in its grotty, rain-soaked undercity. Their arrival is detected by the Face of Boe, who instructs Novice Hame to find the Doctor.

As the Doctor and Martha emerge, various market stalls open up, the stall-holders offering to sell them moods such as Happy, Anger and Mellow. [2] A despondent woman buys Forget; she wants to forget her parents who drove away on the motorway. After she has gone, Martha is grabbed by a young man, Milo, while his partner, Cheen, threatens the Doctor with a gun. [3] They give Martha some Sleep and drag her to their car.

Milo calls the traffic computer to say they have three passengers and it grants them permission to access the fast lane. The Doctor learns from a stall-holder that the car-sharing policy means you can only use the fast lane if you have three adults on board.

Martha awakes. Milo and Cheen explain that Cheen is pregnant and they're heading to Brooklyn where the air smells of apple grass. They say they will drop Martha off when they arrive. It's only 10 miles away – but the journey will take six years. [4]

The Doctor reaches the motorway, gridlocked with hovering cars. He's picked up by a friendly cat-person called Brannigan and his wife, Valerie. They've been on the motorway for 12 years. [5]

Milo, Cheen and Martha descend to the fast lane beneath the traffic jam where the air is thick with exhaust fumes. Cheen has heard stories of cars going missing down there.

The Doctor uses Brannigan's radio to contact the police, but is placed on hold. He calls the Cassini sisters (they're not sisters, they're married) who are able to give him the number of the car that took Martha. [6]

The people stuck in their cars sing *The Old Rugged Cross*. The Doctor decides to reach the fast lane – by dropping through the bottom of Brannigan's car on to the one below. He passes through several cars with eccentric occupants before arriving at one driven by a city gent. He opens the floor to gaze into the fog below and sees giant crabs – the Macra! [7]

Martha, Milo and Cheen discover all the ways off the fast lane are closed and they can't go up again. They swerve between the claws of the Macra. [8]

Hame catches up with the Doctor and they teleport to the Senate building in the city. It is littered with skeletons; the entire population was wiped out by a virus. [9] The Face of Boe sealed the undercity and the motorway to save the inhabitants, keeping things running using his own life force.

The Doctor uses some residual power to open the roof of the motorway and contacts all the cars, ordering them to drive up so his friends can leave the fast lane. They do so and Milo's car flies up into the daylight. [10]

Martha arrives in the Senate to find the Doctor tending to the Face of Boe. The Face of Boe reveals its final secret, telling the Doctor "You are not alone" before it dies. [11]

The Doctor and Martha return to the undercity. The Doctor admits to Martha that he lied about being able to visit his home planet. He explains that it was destroyed, along with the Time Lords, during the Time War. [12]

Pre-production

"**G**ridlock was always going to be about the three levels of New New York," Russell T Davies told *Doctor Who Magazine*. "Up on high, in the overcity, the posh people – who weren't dead, when I first started thinking. Below that, the undercity, with the motorway. And below *that*, at the base of the city, where the concrete meets the sea, the monsters."

In part, *Gridlock* was a sequel to the 2006 episode *New Earth* [see Volume 51] and the Doctor's now-annual visit to the future of the year five billion. "It was always the plan that in the 2007 series, we'd go inside the city," Davies explained in *Doctor Who Magazine*, the gleaming metropolis having only been seen in the distance previously. However, Davies resisted the notion of a direct sequel, preferring – as with *New Earth* – to take some familiar concepts or characters from a previous episode and tell a new story, adding new elements to the mythology. "*Doctor Who*'s strength can be its weakness... the fact that you are in a different place every week and it's very hard to build up a supporting cast and continuity," said Davies on *Doctor Who Confidential*. The new episode was set in 5,000,000,053, some 30 years after events in *New Earth*.

One character that Davies had liked in *New Earth* was Novice Hame, particularly Anna Hope's performance behind the cat prosthetic. "We didn't see enough of her. I wanted her to have some sort of redemption," Davies explained in *Doctor Who Magazine*. This fitted in well with the third and final appearance of the Face of Boe as Hame would now serve as his nurse. Davies had originally planned that Boe would die in *New Earth* having revealed to the Doctor that he was not the last of the Time Lords – thus setting up a narrative for later on – but when the next series had been guaranteed, he shelved this sequence for later use. This added an air of mystery, since in *Dalek* [2005 – see Volume 49] the Doctor had claimed that he would have sensed the survival of any other Time Lords.

One piece of inadvertent continuity came from outside the series itself. In the 2005 book *Doctor Who: Monsters and Villains*, Davies had 'translated' a piece of JB Dane's about the Face of Boe, noting, 'Legend has it that if the Face of Boe should die one day, then the sky will crack asunder. And it is said that he holds one, final secret, that he will speak this secret with his final breath, to one person and one person alone. A homeless, wandering traveller...' In retrospect, this fitted in perfectly with

Below:
With his dying words, the Face of Boe imparts a secret to the Doctor.

the opening of the motorway roof. "I didn't remember I'd written that," admitted Davies on the commentary, "then [*Monsters and Villains* editor] Justin Richards emailed me when he saw the script... although it must have been in my head somewhere."

The Face of Boe's final secret itself had actually been revealed by Davies in August 2005 in his *Meet the Doctor* feature in Panini's *Doctor Who Annual 2006*: 'Far away, across the universe, on the planet Crafe Tec Heydra, one side of a mountain carries carvings and hieroglyphs... The artwork shows two races clashing, one metal, one flesh; a fearsome explosion; and a solitary survivor walking from the wreckage. Solitary? Perhaps not. Under this figure, a phrase has been scratched in the stone, which translates as: *you are not alone...*'

Dark city

While only female cat people had been seen in *New Earth*, Davies wanted to add their male equivalents to the new story. The look of Brannigan – whom Davies wrote with an Irish accent in mind – came from the computer generated character of Ratz who had linked children's BBC programmes from 1994 and appeared in *Live & Kicking*; "A ginger cat with a flying helmet and goggles and scarf... and that's always stuck in my head," explained Davies on the commentary.

For his vision of New New York, Davies drew heavily upon Mega-City One, the huge futuristic East American metropolis policed by Judge Dredd in his many comic appearances since his début in *2000 AD* in 1977. "I was very inspired by Mega-City One: the sheer barminess of the people crammed into a huge, bristling city," explained Davies in *Doctor Who Magazine*, and in the commentary added that he

Above: Brannigan has spent 12 years on the motorway but has travelled just six miles.

loved the city being "full of odd little people with odd little habits".

"It's a dark story. There's a blackness right at the heart of it," he observed on *Doctor Who Confidential*. However, rather than go with a dystopian view of pirates and cannibals preying on those trapped in a violent and unpleasant city, Davies instead opted to show the programme's humanity, depicting likeable characters surviving against adversity, bonded together as a community by their hope and their singing of hymns in the most dismal of circumstances. Originally, Davies had notions for showing the gaudy lifestyle of those in the overcity who were ignoring the horrors unleashed in the motorway, but the events on the nightmarish thoroughfare began to dominate the story, and the writer eliminated the affluent city dwellers and ultimately gave the city to the freed drivers.

Trying to think of a suitable monster originally to have dwelt in the seas of New Earth for the story, Davies

Connections: Bad Wolf

❯ As the Doctor passes through the teenage girls' car, a poster is visible which features a rough translation of 'Bad Wolf' in both Chinese and Japanese. The 'Bad Wolf' meme had featured prominently in the adventures of the Ninth Doctor [see Volumes 48-50].

'RUSSELL T DAVIES OPTED TO
SHOW THE PROGRAMME'S HUMANITY,
DEPICTING LIKEABLE CHARACTERS
SURVIVING AGAINST ADVERSITY.'

considered various colossal menaces along the lines of Japan's famous cinematic mutant dinosaur Godzilla, a huge octopus, and eventually the notion of giant crabs. Giant crustaceans called the Macra had previously appeared in the 1967 serial *The Macra Terror* [see Volume 10] written by Ian Stuart Black, and as Davies explained on *Totally Doctor Who*, "I might as well honour the old monster and name it after them."

Davies recalled *The Macra Terror* from its original broadcast and was delighted to pay homage to one of the forgotten monsters from the Patrick Troughton era of the programme, even if he had to turn the Macra into brainless beasts in the intervening billions of years. "I always imagined that when New New York had been flourishing, they'd been kept in the City Zoo, and when everyone died, they escaped and settled in the fog, like those fabled alligators," he explained in *Doctor Who Magazine* with reference to the New York reptile legends of the 1930s.

Jumping the queue

"I just thought it was cute for once to bring back one that nobody would remember," explained Davies on *Doctor Who Confidential*, "I thought it was a nice change to revive an old enemy, to portray it in CGI and to bring it back to life." Having checked with visual effects company, The Mill that such creatures were feasible, Davies developed the notion of red baby Macra eating the occupants of the cars on the lowest level of the motorway, with the Doctor finding skeletons and tiny crabs inside the vehicles. He would then emerge from the motorway on to a concrete ledge to find huge adult Macra rising from the sea which would pursue him up the city walls, terrorising the inhabitants. Rather than drop the

Left:
The Doctor makes his own way down to the bottom of the motorway.

Macra when eliminating the overcity dwellers and the sea from his story, Davies reasoned that since, in *The Macra Terror,* the giant aliens had originally lived on gas, the choking exhaust emissions of the cars now at the centre of his story would be a perfect environment for them. However, the way that the Macra were used meant that prior information about them was not needed by the audience to enjoy the story.

"I wanted to do a story where they're living within the CGI," explained Davies on the commentary, "the ultimate integration of the whole thing." The creation of the motorway – the environment inside which most of the story is acted out – was fundamental to the script, and also gave the setting for one of the episode's main set pieces. "The car jumping sequence is one of my favourite things," said Davies on *Doctor Who Confidential*. "To have the Doctor going up and down as opposed to across the cars just gives it a size and a scale that you can't often get on television."

Pharmacy Alley came about when Davies realised that a grim, dark alley was a location

Connections: Sing-along

▶ The hymn sung by the travellers is *The Old Rugged Cross,* a gospel song written in 1912 by the evangelist George Bennard. The song was published in 1915 and became a popular part of several evangelistic campaigns. The first commercial recording of the song was made in 1921.

Connections:
Picture this
▶ The Ma and Pa couple seen in the car in the opening scene are dressed as the couple depicted in Grant Wood's famous 1930 oil painting *American Gothic*.

which, though easy to achieve with some simple set dressing in South Wales, could also echo the exaggerated urban look of *2000 AD*. The notion of the emotion or forgetfulness-inducing drugs was inspired by the mood-creating chemicals in Gareth Roberts' Ninth Doctor novel *Only Human,* published in September 2005.

In terms of the Doctor and Martha's developing relationship, on *Doctor Who Confidential* Davies observed, "The episode... starts out with [the Doctor's] normal, private, closed self. Then... [Martha]'s lost. She's in a strange world. He brought her there on a whim. He was showing off. He was going back to places he used to take Rose and he feels guilty because of that."

Gridlock was to be made alongside *The Lazarus Experiment* [2007 – see page 88] as part of the third recording block under the direction of Richard Clark, a new talent for *Doctor Who* who had been spotted by executive producer Julie Gardner having just helmed two episodes of *Life on Mars*. The tone meeting for the episode was held at the meeting room of Upper Boat on the morning of Wednesday 16 August 2006,

and as a result of the various discussions, Davies spent the next day revising the script. The look of the city was influenced very much by *Blade Runner* and the cities of other science-fiction films such as the futuristic New York seen in the 1997 movie *The Fifth Element* and the *Star Wars* films (notably Coruscant in 2002's *Attack of the Clones*). The concept drawings were produced by Sarah Payne of the BBC design department. The Mill had already designed a version of New New York for *New Earth* which influenced the look of the cars.

The third draft script of Monday 4 September effectively formed the shooting script for *Gridlock* issued on Wednesday 6. Sally Calypso was described as "blonde, beautiful and smiling" and originally commented that she was "sponsored by Eeze-E-Bone, to soothe aches and pains"; the holographic reporter was inspired by Swifty Frisko, a reporter from the 1984 comic strip *The Ballad of Halo Jones* in *2000 AD*.

Memories of home

The interior of Ma and Pa's vehicle was described as 'the interior of a car, though maybe three times the size. Front windscreen, side windows, but outside them, only a dirty yellow mist. The whole interior is scuffed, lived-in, poor. Black metal walls & upholstery; it's a dark, cramped little box. Futuristic, but not flash, little lights and switches everywhere, every surface studded'. Ma and Pa were 'mid-50s, thin, very scared'.

Talking to Martha about his home planet, the Doctor described the sky as a burnt orange (mentioned by the Doctor's granddaughter Susan in the 1964 serial *The Sensorites* [see Volume 3]), the Citadel enclosed in a mighty glass dome (first illustrated in the masthead

Below: Novice Hame took care of the Face of Boe for 24 years as penance for her past sins.

to the *Gallifrey Guardian* news pages in *Doctor Who Magazine* in 1980), grass (the 1996 TV Movie *Doctor Who* [see Volume 47]), and mountains capped with snow (to which the Doctor had alluded in the 1972 story *The Time Monster* [see Volume 18]); later he added that the leaves on the trees were silver (*The Sensorites* again) and it was stated for the first time that Gallifrey had twin suns. Novice Hame 'a Human Cat (from *New Earth*)' was 'now older, greyer, wearing a dark version of her Sister's clothes' and the stage directions noted 'she's a different cat now, no longer innocent'. In Pharmacy Alley, the Pharmacy Booths were 'like burger vans in a city-centre at night', and the script noted that on the screen, the Doctor and Martha should see 'the FX SHOT view of New New York as seen in *New Earth*' (indeed, various CGI sequences from the earlier episode would feature on screens in the finished show), with Martha deducing that the Doctor had visited this place before, with Rose. The first Pharmacist was '30, in grubby white uniform' while the customer was a young woman, 'early 20s, drab clothes, pale, a shawl over her head.' Milo and Cheen were 'both early 20s [in] rough denim/combat gear'. Describing the exterior of Milo and Cheen's car in the wider alleyway, Davies noted, 'assume one prac[tical] build for the exterior Cars, if possible? Not especially futuristic, like a big, black, bulky, boxy, SUV, but with no wheels.'

Real New York landmarks were referred to, such as Battery Park in South Manhattan, the borough of Brooklyn and its neighbourhood of Flatlands, and the major Manhattan intersection of Times Square (now New Times Square). Describing the motorway, Davies' script outlined 'a mile-wide circular concrete tunnel. Cars, suspended in the air, all identical, in 20 lanes of traffic. And 50 lanes *deep*... The air yellow, dirty.' The writer later noted, 'if windscreens are dirty yellow, they can stay opaque from the outside, to save matting drivers & passengers into exterior shots of Cars'. Thomas Kincade Brannigan was first described as 'a man in goggles, flying-helmet, leather jacket & scarf' and then revealed to be 'a Human Cat, 40s, a roguish Ginger Tom' with Valerie introduced as '30, shrewd'. The Doctor also remarked that he met the Duke of Manhattan, seen in *New Earth*. The Cassinis, Alice and May, were described as 'two 70 y/o women'. When the rendition of *The Old Rugged Cross* began in Brannigan's car, the stage directions indicated that the Doctor was moved by this; 'he reaches out, as an apology, clasps Valerie on the shoulder, which she accepts; comforting her'.

Above:
The Doctor is unhappy to find 'moods' being sold in the lower depths of New New York.

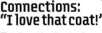

**Connections:
"I love that coat!"**

❯ When the Doctor leaves his long coat behind in Brannigan's car, he comments that he was given it by 1960s American blues-rock singer Janis Joplin.

Connections: In the name of...

▶ Several of the characters in the story make reference to 'Jehovah', which is the proper name of the God of Israel as given in the Hebrew Bible.

This action was the subject of debate during rehearsals and ultimately dropped. "We talked about whether that was right or not," said David Tennant on the DVD episode commentary, and Davies agreed with the actor's reasoning that it was the hymn that triggered the Doctor into action rather than accepting the situation as the motorists had. The writer had chosen *The Old Rugged Cross* to demonstrate the notion of faith, irrespective of any belief in a deity.

In the first car that the Doctor entered on leaving Brannigan's was a 'bright white man (like the one in *New Earth*)' and then later 'a formal, suited 40 y/o Businessman in bowler-hat'. The Businessman was directly inspired by Max Normal, one of Judge Dredd's best informants, first appearing in the early days of the *2000 AD* strip and always clad in a pinstriped suit and bowler hat, complete with carnation.

Javit was 'a scrawny black female cat'. As the Doctor looked down out of the Businessman's car he saw, 'huge, slow, lumbering 60-foot crabs. Massive

crustaceans, a bed of them, piled on top of each other, with small, bright, white shining eyes on stalks. The topmost creatures slowly wave their 20ft front claws... The claws snap lazily, with that terrible sound.' Martha's idea of turning everything in the car off so that it could not be detected by the Macra was a notion she recalled from submarine films – a stealth technique called 'silent running'. In the remains of the Senate, the Doctor originally scanned one of the crumbling skeletons with his sonic screwdriver. As Novice Hame knelt beside the dying Face of Boe, the script described the scene as 'like a portrait of a Victorian lament'. The script concluded with the singing of *Abide With Me*, a Christian hymn composed by Henry Lyte in 1847, sung to William Monk's melody *Eventide*; "One of the most beautiful songs ever written," said Russell T Davies on the commentary, while in the book *The Writer's Tale* adding: 'I didn't write *Gridlock* thinking this is my take on religion. My foremost thought, and my principal job, was to write an entertaining drama about cats and humans stuck on a motorway.' The pre-credits took place on 'Day A', along with the Face of Boe's realisation that the Doctor was coming. The remainder of the episode then took place on 'Day 5', which for the Doctor and Martha was immediately after her first trip in the TARDIS during *The Shakespeare Code* [2007 – see Volume 54].

Guest stars

Another tone meeting was held at Upper Boat on Tuesday 5 September, after which recces for Block Three were held on Thursday 7 and Friday 8 September, concurrent with the recording of *The Shakespeare Code*. A production meeting was then held on the

Below:
The Doctor invades a car on the motorway bottom and discovers the horrible truth.

Above:
Milo, Martha
and Cheen find
themselves
the prey of
the Macra!

Friday afternoon at the Holland House Hotel to discuss venues and other matters.

Of the guest cast for the episode, topping the bill as Brannigan was Ardal O'Hanlon, an Irish comedy actor best known for the sitcoms *Father Ted* and *My Hero*. "When I was asked to do *Doctor Who*, first of all I was hoping to be a baddie. I was slightly disappointed that Brannigan wasn't more malicious," O'Hanlon told *Doctor Who Confidential*. The actor knew the series and was aware of *New Earth* and the cat people as Davies recalled in *Doctor Who Magazine*: "I didn't need to give him any back-story, he was fully versed." Anna Hope reprised her role as Novice Hame for a second time since *New Earth*, having donned her feline prosthetic for the accompanying Tardisode on Tuesday 31 January. Playing Valerie, Jennifer Hennessy had appeared in Russell T Davies' drama *The Second Coming*, while Georgine Anderson had previously played a character called May in another of Davies' productions, his 1993 BBC children's serial *Century Falls*. Alice was played by Bridget Turner, wife of Frank Cox who had directed episodes of *Doctor Who* in 1964 including the final two parts of the serial *The Sensorites*. Playing the Pale Lady was Lucy Davenport, and returning as the voice of the Face of Boe, as in *New Earth*, was Struan Rodger.

The readthrough for the episode was held at the Holland House Hotel on the evening of Monday 11 September following recording on *The Shakespeare Code* for David Tennant and Freema Agyeman. Pink amendments to the script on Wednesday 13 September covered the TARDIS' arrival in New New York, Martha's kidnapping, the Doctor talking to the Businessman, the scene with Martha contemplating her death in Milo and Cheen's car, the Doctor telling the drivers to "drive up!" A minor change to one of Sally Calypso's announcements in Brannigan's car was made as a blue amendment on Friday 15 September. ■

'DURING HIS DEATH SCENE, THE FACE OF BOE SPOKE HIS FINAL SECRET WITH HIS MOUTH RATHER THAN TELEPATHICALLY.'

Production

Recording for Block Three and *Gridlock* began on Monday 18 September, the week after the bulk of *The Shakespeare Code* had been recorded. The venue for the first couple of days was the Temple of Peace in the Cathays Park area of Cardiff, first used by the *Doctor Who* team in October 2004 for the recording of *The End of the World* [2005 – see Volume 48]. Because most of the sequences for the episode were interiors

or set during daytime, the production schedule most days was a steady 8am to 7pm without the need for night shoots. Erika Macleod recorded her reports as the holographic Sally Calypso first, after which some sequences between Hame and the Face of Boe were recorded in the Darkened Temple. Sarah Lockwood of Millennium FX was on hand to transform Anna Hope into an older version of her feline character (with a new flock fur pattern and colouring), while Rob Mayor and Gustav Hoegen were on hand from the same company to operate the Face of Boe, the dialogue for whom was read in on a temporary basis by first assistant director Dan Mumford. While Freema Agyeman was not required, David Tennant was needed for the sequence where Hame explained that the city had died. David also spent the day recording a video diary for BBC Worldwide, chatting to Anna Hope on location.

Back at the Temple the next day, the cast was joined by Freema Agyeman for most of the remaining Darkened Temple scenes. When the glass started to break on the Face of Boe's casing, it was originally planned to record the Doctor giving instructions to the cars to fly upwards while the glass was removed, after which the death scene would be played – but scheduling issues led to the Doctor's inserts being deferred. During his death scene, the Face of Boe spoke his final secret with his mouth rather than telepathically; this was at the request of Neill Gorton of Millennium because the prop's mouth mechanism had been improved for *New Earth* but never used. "On the day of Boe's death scene, David actually texted me from set, to say how ridiculously sad it was! A great big lump of animatronic latex, and everyone felt sorry for him!" commented Davies to *Doctor Who Magazine*.

Freema Agyeman was now released for three days and returned to London where she presented the Best Group Award at the MOBOs on Wednesday 20 September. Meanwhile, David Tennant worked at Upper Boat where the standard car set had been constructed in Studio 6. This basic modular set, made by an external company called Icon, was economic because it could be re-dressed as many different vehicles during production, but started off as Brannigan's car for the scenes of the Doctor's entry into the vehicle, as well

as later scenes with Brannigan and Valerie plus Hame's arrival (with stunt arranger Crispin Layfield supervising Anna Hope's entrance). "It was a tricky set to film on because it's wee," Tennant told viewers of *Doctor Who Confidential*. After much debate, it was decided not to show the images outside the car windows clearly, as with Captain Jack's ship in the 2005 episode *The Empty Child* [see Volume 50]; instead, fake fumes were generated and two red lights on a stick waved by a crew member represented the rear of the vehicle in front.

Rockwood Animals provided six kittens as the couple's children, and quite some time was devoted trying to get one of the animals to move its mouth so that The Mill could create the illusion of one of them mewing "Mama" to Valerie. As Richard Clark commented, "We went for a slightly random approach, where we pointed the camera… and had various people shouting and screaming and waving food around

**Connections
Face off**

▶ The Doctor first encountered the Face of Boe in *The End of the World* [2005 – see Volume 48] on Platform One while in his ninth incarnation. After regenerating into his tenth body, their next meeting was in New New York in *New Earth* [2006 – see Volume 51].

Right:
The Doctor says hello to one of Brannigan and Valerie's offspring.

Above:
Ardal O'Hanlon
as Brannigan
prepares for his
close-up.

until hopefully one of them did something we could use." Work was witnessed by a crew from *Doctor Who Confidential* (which covered John Cormican's transformation of O'Hanlon into Brannigan, with the prosthetics made from a cast of the actor's face), and also a web interactive team headed by Claire Jones.

In close quarters

Work began on Thursday 21 September with a photoshoot deferred from the previous evening to show Alice and May in their younger days as displayed on Brannigan's monitor. Following this were some of the scenes with Brannigan and Valerie held over from the previous day, after which other material in Brannigan's car covered the Doctor calling the police, the singing of *The Old Rugged Cross* (for which the cast wore hidden earpieces so that they could hear a library playback of the song) and the Doctor's decision to descend to the fast lane. Scheduled on set for this recording were representatives from the publications *Doctor Who Adventures* and *SFX*.

The main scenes in Brannigan's car were completed on Friday 22 September,

wrapping up a couple of scenes held over from the previous day, before David Tennant and Ardal O'Hanlon recorded the greenscreen shots of Brannigan urging the Doctor into the safety of his car. Tennant then recorded the scenes in the Businessman's car – swiftly re-dressed from Brannigan's car while the greenscreen material was being recorded – before departing for a long weekend. Freema returned to the shoot on Saturday 23 September, where the car set had been refitted to represent Milo and Cheen's vehicle for the recording of the early scenes with Martha and her rather amiable kidnappers. The three actors would spend a couple of days in these close quarters. "It really helped that I got on like wildfire with Travis Oliver and Lenora Crichlow," Freema told *Doctor Who Magazine*. "It was a really enclosed set and there were just the three of us, in each other's faces all the time. It could have been a nightmare, but I really enjoyed myself." As it turned out, Freema and Travis were both big fans of the animated sitcom *The*

Connections:
Time's arrow

❯ For the Doctor and Martha, *Gridlock* takes place immediately after *The Shakespeare Code* [2007 – see Volume 54], with the Doctor seen removing the arrow which had impacted on the TARDIS door at the end of their previous adventure.

Right:
David Tennant performs against greenscreen for the Doctor's descent from car to car.

Simpsons and spent a lot of time between takes challenging each other to guess quotes from episodes.

The crew stood down for a one-day weekend on Sunday 24 September. Then on Monday 25, it was back to work in Milo and Cheen's car with Any Effects providing the buckling and caving in of the walls during the Macra attack in the later scenes, all covered by *Doctor Who Confidential*; the impact of the creatures on the car was simulated by first assistant director Dan Mumford banging the side of the vehicle. Tennant rejoined the cast the next day when the car had been refurbished into the homely abode of the Cassinis and, after the scenes with the ladies had been recorded, he performed the opening TARDIS scene with Freema as the design team hurriedly refurbished the vehicle as that of the Red Man, and then finally as Whitey's car. This time, not only was *Doctor Who Confidential* on hand to speak to the crew, but interviews were also conducted for BMI's in-flight magazine to give an insight about working on *Doctor Who*.

Of the main cast, only David Tennant and Nicholas Boulton were required for Wednesday 27, which began with the Doctor's passage through the teenage girls' car after which the set was restored to that of the Businessman's car for a couple of previously deferred solo scenes. While the car was then being re-dressed for the naked couple, *Doctor Who Confidential* covered the greenscreen work of the Doctor dropping from vehicle to vehicle in the motorway. In the effects area, a vehicle base had been built on scaffolding ten feet above an entire prop car, with Tennant only having to drop around four feet from one car to another. In the afternoon, a closed set was enforced for the brief naked interlude encountered by the Doctor in his journey, after which David performed pick-up shots of his orders to the motorists on a partial Darkened Temple mock-up in Studio 5 along with close-ups of the Face of Boe. This was followed by some effects shots from Brannigan's car and the Businessman's car, plus shots of the Doctor coming through a generic car hatch back in Studio 6.

Last day on set

To conclude work on *Gridlock*, the crew was due to spend two more days on location doing the alley scenes in Cardiff Bay at the disused industrial warehouse venue of The Maltings on East Tyndall Street which was being converted into an atrium for an office block. The unit was warned that they would need wet weather gear for work on Thursday 28 September which would see Any Effects creating rain to drench David Tennant, Freema Agyeman and the rest of the cast on the cold location between 9am and 8pm. With the police controlling traffic in the area around the shoot, BBC Publicity and *Doctor Who Confidential* were both on set to cover the Doctor and Martha's

---

Connections:
Secret message

▶ The Face of Boe tells the Doctor, "You are not alone." The truth behind this cryptic comment is revealed in the episode *Utopia* [2007 - see Volume 56] when the Doctor discovers that he is not the only surviving Time Lord.

arrival by TARDIS, Martha's kidnap (with stunt arranger Tom Lucy supervising the action sequence) and the Doctor talking to the Pharmacists. When lighting the area, director of photography Rory Taylor went for a style reminiscent of the 1982 science-fiction movie *Blade Runner*, with its depiction of a Los Angeles of 2019; "I wanted to make it look sinister, in a real contrast to the New New York we saw in *New Earth*," he told *Doctor Who Magazine*. The *New Earth* medical logo of the green crescent was also in evidence, and a video screen was placed to relay the Sally Calypso announcements. The arrival scene was completed on Friday 29 along with the Doctor's speech to Martha at the end of the programme. Following this, the crew relocated to the Ely Papermill in Cardiff, first used as the Nestene lair in *Rose* [2005 – see Volume 48] in August 2004, where *Doctor Who Confidential* covered the sequence of the Doctor following the kidnap party.

The final day of recording on *Gridlock* was back at Upper Boat on Monday 2 October and did not feature either David or Freema, who were out on location working with the rest of the Jones family on *Smith and Jones* [2007 – see Volume 54] (the scenes being scheduled because the Jones clan were due to feature heavily in *The Lazarus Experiment* which started taping next day). The pre-credit sequence in Ma and Pa's car was recorded first. After the vehicle was re-dressed, the scenes in Javit's vehicle were recorded; here Rob Mayor handled Daisy Lewis' prosthetic as Javit while Any Effects provided the ripping walls as the car was attacked. Finally came various effects shots of Brannigan's exhaust and some viewscreen shots in the Generic car, after which Richard Clark and his crew focused on *The Lazarus Experiment*.

At the end of Block Three, further second unit inserts were recorded for *Gridlock* at Upper Boat on Wednesday 18 October; these included a remount of the Doctor passing through the Naked Car, shots of Novice Hame's bangle with an arm double, and a shot of the patch being passed to the Pale Woman. Inserts of Sally Calypso in the viewscreen were also recorded at Upper Boat on Tuesday 7 November. ■

PRODUCTION

Mon 18 Sep 06 Welsh Centre for International Affairs, Temple of Peace, College Road, Cardiff (TV Studio: Darkened Temple)

Tue 19 Sep 06 Welsh Centre for International Affairs (Darkened Temple)

Wed 20 - Thu 21 Sep 06 Upper Boat Studios, Trefforest: Studio 6 (Brannigan's Car)

Fri 22 Sep 06 Upper Boat Studios: Studio 6 (Brannigan's Car; Motorway Platform; Motorway Corridor; Businessman's Car)

Sat 23, Mon 25 Sep 06 Upper Boat Studios: Studio 6 (Milo & Cheen's Car)

Tue 26 Sep 06 Upper Boat Studios: Studio 6 (Cassinis' Car; TARDIS; Red Man's Car; White's Car)

Wed 27 Sep 06 Upper Boat Studios: Studio 6 (Teenage Girls' Car; Businessman's Car; Motorway (Car Roof); Naked Car; Brannigan's Car; Generic Car); Studio 5 (Darkened Temple)

Thu 28 Sep 06 The Maltings, East Tyndall Street, Cardiff Bay (Alleyway; Pharmacy Alley)

Fri 29 Sep 06 The Maltings (Alleyway; Pharmacy Alley; Wider Alleyway); Unit 7, Ely Papermill, Sanatorium Road, Cardiff (Warehouses)

Mon 2 Oct 06 Upper Boat Studios: Studio 6 (Ma & Pa's Car; Javit's Car; Brannigan's Car; Generic Car)

Wed 18 Oct 06 Upper Boat Studios (Naked Car; Businessman's Car; Darkened Temple; Brannigan's Car; Generic Car; Pharmacy Alley)

Tue 7 Nov 06 Upper Boat Studios (viewscreen)

Main image:
Concept art for
the New New
York motorway.

Post-production

The episode – formally entitled *Gridlock* late in the day, although it had always been referred to by this title – featured a great deal of CGI work, with particularly heavy usage in the motorway sequences. Three different versions of the 3D cars were created at different resolutions, taking about three weeks' work. Having looked at photographs of the original Macra, The Mill developed a variation where the aliens had devolved to make them bigger and less intelligent. An initial design was felt to be too sleek and futuristic, so visual FX supervisor Dave Houghton made this into a rougher type of spider-crab. The Mill also provided shots of the huge atrium, the crack running across the Face of Boe's tank, and the interior and exterior matte shots of the Senate House. Cloud footage was obtained from World Backgrounds at Elstree to be seen through the car windscreens as they flew up into the sky. Late in proceedings, the team decided that a clearer shot depicting the Macra was needed, with producer Phil Collinson squeezing the budget to allow The Mill to add this extra effect.

The producer and director credits were superimposed over the opening TARDIS scene. In the pre-credits, when Ma berated Pa for lying to the computer, he originally replied, "I know, and I'm sorry, sweetheart, I only wanted to get you home." A short scene immediately after the opening credits showing the Face of Boe in the Darkened Temple was cut; this had the telepathic voice saying, "He is coming." This was effectively replaced

Right:
Let's face it - it's the end for the Face of Boe.

by the Face's "he has arrived", added in post-production, during the next scene with Hame where he had originally noted, "The creatures are stirring, in the depths." The end of the scene where Milo and Cheen were granted access to the fast lane originally had Milo telling Cheen, "We're gonna get there, sweetheart. Just sit back, we're gonna find a home. A brand-new home." In the next scene in the car when Martha comes to, Milo was originally on the radio saying, "...repeat, Car 4-6-5-diamond-6, heading for the fast lane, drivepath computer on a 5-to-1 descent pattern, thank you very much."

Old friends

When Brannigan remarked to Valerie that the Doctor seemed a bit slow, his wife responded, "Oh, I think he's the opposite." A voice-over with Milo descending to the fast lane was omitted from one motorway effects shot, and when Martha remarked sarcastically that 30 miles an hour was crazy, Cheen commented, "Oh, he's got a wild side, has Milo," and added that in the back they also had "plenty of vids and music and games". When the Doctor grabbed the microphone to ask the Cassinis about Martha, Alice responded, "Who've you got there, Brannigan, some sort of idiot? Get lost out there, and you stay lost." When May confirmed that the car containing Martha had gone down to the fast lane, Alice originally added, "They'll have gone down, that's all we can know. Deep down." The scene of the Doctor contacting the Cassinis was cut in two and placed either side of a sequence with Martha. When the Doctor contacted the women again, May explained to him, "We're heading for the Flatlands." "There are houses out there, made of wood," added Alice, "And

Above: The Doctor joins the family Brannigan on their slow journey to nowhere.

cinnamon wheat, reaching all the way to the horizon."

When Javit called Milo and Cheen, she originally asked their names. After Novice Hame told the Doctor about the mutated virus, he originally asked, "Are we safe?" to which she replied, "Oh, it's dead, now." After Martha started talking to Milo and Cheen about the Doctor, Cheen said, "He was tall. I like 'em tall." "Oy, watch it," said Milo, smiling.

For the end of the episode, Murray Gold originally wrote a new hymn, a wordless piece with choir voices which echoed the incidental score for the episode. However, beautiful though it was, it was felt that, *Abide With Me* was more apt.

Additional dialogue recording for the episode took place at Air Studios on Tuesday 13 February 2007, while an additional line from the Doctor covering Martha's reaction to seeing cat people was also added in post-production. Another late change was the dying Face of Boe referring to the Doctor as "old friend" because – since recording the episode – Russell T Davies had decided that the series' climax would imply that the Face of Boe was actually the Doctor's friend, Captain Jack Harkness. ■

Publicity

Martha is a victim of road-rage!

▶ Comments by Russell T Davies in an issue of *Doctor Who Magazine* were taken out of context and became newsworthy, with BBC News reporting on Tuesday 19 September 2006 that "budgetary constraints" would keep the series "largely Earthbound" – a reference to Davies having noted that if alien worlds were produced unconvincingly, this would lead to bad reviews. The story was taken up by tabloids like the *Daily Star* while the one-minute news on BBC Three that day incorrectly claimed the Doctor would not leave Earth at all this series.

▶ In the week leading up to transmission of *Gridlock*, *Radio Times* ran a one-page feature called *Cat and Doc* in its *Doctor Who Watch* slot in which Will Cohen of The Mill outlined how the sequence with the Doctor dropping from one car to another was achieved. Mark Braxton selected *Gridlock* as one of *Today's Choices* noting that the episode 'accelerates to its finishing line with important revelations' as well as complimenting the effects work. In the letters column, Eve Lockett of Abingdon noted the similarities between the lead characters in *Smith and Jones* and ITV1's adaptation of Jane Austen's *Persuasion* which had screened on Sunday 1 April, while 12-year-old Charlie Ibrahim-Rogers of Beccles commented that his apprehension at the loss of Billie Piper vanished with the 'fantastic' performance of Freema as Martha.

▶ Because of the BBC One coverage of an FA Cup semi-final on *Match of the Day Live*, *Gridlock* was scheduled in the later slot of 7.40pm, with a proviso that if the football went into extra time the episode would be postponed to Saturday 21 April. This actually became a news story from the BBC on Wednesday 11, with the Corporation indicating that if *Gridlock* was not shown, *Rose* would replace *Doctor Who Confidential* on BBC Three and, *The Christmas Invasion* would fill the slot of both the repeat of *Gridlock* and *Doctor Who Confidential Cut Down* on Sunday.

▶ A *Blue Peter* feature on Chris Collins giving the grounds of the Royal Marsden Hospital a *Doctor Who* makeover had been scheduled for transmission on Thursday 12 April, but in fact was screened a day early. On Friday 13, *Doctor Who* fan and comic songster Mitch Benn delivered a song on Radio 4's *The Now Show* which implored Manchester United to quickly beat Watford to prevent the cancellation of *Gridlock*; this was subsequently released on CD in 2010 as part of *Doctor at the BBC: A Legend Reborn*.

MIND YOUR HEAD

"RADIO TIMES RAN A ONE-PAGE
FEATURE CALLED CAT AND DOC."

Broadcast

▶ *Doctor Who* fans breathed a sigh of relief when it seemed that Manchester United had the upper hand over Watford and, at half-time during *Match of the Day Live*, BBC One screened a trailer for *Gridlock* with presenter Gary Lineker then welcoming viewers "back to the TARDIS". With a 4-1 victory evident, extra time at Villa Park was averted and *Gridlock* went out as planned, with the continuity announcer saying it followed after "travel news with Sally Calypso". *Gridlock* got almost double the audience of *Who Wants to Be a Millionaire?* on ITV1. The corresponding episode of *Doctor Who Confidential*, *Are We There Yet?*, aired at 8.45pm on BBC Three, with a *Cutdown* version screened after the two repeats later in the week.

Above right: The Doctor defeats the football coverage.

Below: "Happy, Happy, lovely happy Happy!"

▶ An online commentary for the episode was recorded by Russell T Davies, David Tennant and Dave Houghton of The Mill. In addition to the usual BBC Three repeats at 8pm on Sunday 15 (the channel's top-rated show of the week) and 9pm the following Friday, *Gridlock* was screened on BBC Four at 8.15pm on Tuesday 21 August 2007 as part of an evening of programmes about motoring and motorways.

▶ "There's a fundamental optimism that things are going to get better," said Davies of *Gridlock*, "You could see it as very sad and lost and lonely, in that they are singing in the dark, and if the Doctor hadn't come along, nothing would save them. But actually they're right to have hope; the Doctor *does* come along..."

ORIGINAL TRANSMISSION

EPISODE	DATE	TIME	CHANNEL	DURATION	RATING (CHART POSITION)	APPRECIATION INDEX
Gridlock	Saturday 14 April 2007	7.40pm-8.25pm	BBC One	44'58"	8.41M (7th)	86

Merchandise

Gridlock was initially released on DVD by 2|entertain in May 2007 along with *Smith and Jones* and *The Shakespeare Code* as *Series 3 Volume 1*. It was also included in *The Complete Third Series* DVD box set released in November 2007 with a commentary track featuring Julie Gardner, Travis Oliver and visual FX producer Marie Jones recorded a few weeks after transmission. Also included was the episode's original network trailer, the short version of *Doctor Who Confidential* and a sequence from *David Tennant's Video Diary*.

Several tracks of music from *Gridlock* were included on Silva Screen's CD of *Doctor Who: Original Television Soundtrack: Series 3* released in November 2007, including *Abide With Me*. Two tracks of music from *Gridlock* were also included in Silva Screen's limited edition *Doctor Who:*

The TARDIS Edition which was released in November 2014 and the company's earlier four-disc set *The 50th Anniversary Collection* in December 2013.

Character Options released a 5" action figure of Brannigan and both a 5" and a 12" figure of Novice Hame. ∎

Above left:
The soundtrack album for the 2007 series.

Left:
One of the Novice Hame action figures.

Below left:
Novice Hame takes a break between takes, as recorded in *Doctor Who Confidential*.

Below:
David Tennant tells all in his *Video Diary*.

Cast and credits

CAST

David Tennant ....The Doctor
Freema Agyeman ....Martha Jones
with
Ardal O'Hanlon ....Brannigan
Anna Hope ....Novice Hame
Travis Oliver ....Milo
Lenora Crichlow ....Cheen
Jennifer Hennessy ....Valerie
Bridget Turner ....Alice
Georgine Anderson ....May
Simon Pearsall ....Whitey
Daisy Lewis ....Javit
Nicholas Boulton ....Businessman
Erika Macleod ....Sally Calypso
Judy Norman ....Ma
Graham Padden ....Pa
Lucy Davenport ....Pale Woman
Tom Edden ....Pharmacist #1[1]
Natasha Williams ....Pharmacist #2[1]
Gayle Telfer Stevens ....Pharmacist #3[1]
Struan Rodger ....The Face of Boe[1]

[1] Not credited in *Radio Times*

UNCREDITED

Naomi Hayama, Kaman Chan ....
....Teenage Cyber Punks
Chris Ilston ....Naked Lad
Grainne Jougin ....Naked Girl
Andrew Cameron ....Red Man
Holly Dymock, Hayley Jones ....Vestal Virgins
**Nina Kitt, Paul Ganney, Stephen Bracken-
Keogh, Daryl Adcock, Lauren Bracewell,
Wendi Sheard, Jenny Pink, Nicholas Wilkes**
.... Crowd ADR

CREDITS

Written by Russell T Davies
Produced by Phil Collinson
Directed by Richard Clark

Macra created by Ian Stuart Black
1st Assistant Director: Dan Mumford
2nd Assistant Director: Jennie Fava [uncredited: Steffan Morris]
3rd Assistant Director: Sarah Davies
Location Manager: Lowri Thomas
Unit Manager: Rhys Griffiths [uncredited: Huw Jones]
Production Co-ordinator: Jess van Niekerk
Production Secretary: Kevin Myers
Production Assistant: Debi Griffiths
Production Runner: Siân Eve Goldsmith [uncredited: Graham Huxtable]
Floor Runners: Lowri Denman, Heddi Joy Taylor
Contracts Assistant: Bethan Britton
Continuity: Non Eleri Hughes
Script Editor: Simon Winstone
Focus Puller: Steve Rees [uncredited: Ant Hugill, Marc Covington, Mari Yamamura , Duncan Fowlie]
Grip: John Robinson [uncredited: Ron Nicholls]
Boom Operator: Jon Thomas [uncredited: Kevin Staples]
Gaffer: Mark Hutchings [uncredited: Steve Slocombe]
Best Boy: Peter Chester
Stunt Co-ordinators: Tom Lucy, Crispin Layfield
Chief Supervising Art Director: Stephen Nicholas
Art Department Production Manager: Jonathan Marquand Allison
Art Dept Co-ordinator: Matthew North
Chief Props Master: Adrian Anscombe
Supervising Art Director: Arwel Wyn Jones
Associate Designer: James North
Set Decorator: Malin Lindholm
Standby Art Director: Leonie Rintler
Design Assistants: Ian Bunting, Al Roberts
Cyfle Trainee: Christian Ibell
Storyboard Artist: Shaun Williams
Standby Props: Phil Shellard, Nick Murray

Standby Carpenter: Paul Jones
Standby Painter: Ellen Woods
Standby Rigger: Bryan Griffiths
Props Master: Paul Aitken
Props Buyer: Blaanid Maddrell
Props Chargehand: Gareth Jeanne
Props Storeman: Martin Griffiths
Forward Dresser: Amy Chandler
Practical Electrician: Albert James
Construction Manager: Matthew Hywel-Davies
Graphics: BBC Wales Graphics
Assistant Costume Designer: Marnie Ormiston
Costume Supervisor: Lindsay Bonaccorsi
Costume Assistants: Sheenagh O'Marah, Kirsty
    Wilkinson [uncredited: Angela Jones, Susie Lewis,
    Ian Chapman]
Make-Up Artists: Pam Mullins, Steve Smith,
    John Munro [uncredited: Ros Wilkins]
Casting Associate: Andy Brierley
Assistant Editors: Ceres Doyle, Tim Hodges
Post-production Supervisors: Chris Blatchford,
    Samantha Hall
Post-production Co-ordinator: Marie Brown
Special Effects Co-ordinator: Ben Ashmore
Special Effects Supervisor: Paul Kelly
Prosthetics Designer: Neill Gorton
Prosthetics Supervisor: Rob Mayor
On Line Editor: Matthew Clarke
Colourist: Mick Vincent
3D Artists: Matthew McKinney, Neil Roche, Jean-
    Claude Deguara, Bruce Magroune, Nick Webber,
    Paul Burton, Jeff North, Serena Cacciato
2D Artists: Sara Bennett, Adam Rowland,
    Tim Barter

Visual Effects Co-ordinators: Rebecca Johnson,
    Jenna Powell
Digital Matte Painter: Simon Wicker
On Set VFX Supervisor: Barney Curnow
Dubbing Mixer: Tim Ricketts
Supervising Sound Editor: Paul McFadden
Sound Editor: Doug Sinclair
Sound FX Editor: Paul Jefferies
Finance Manager: Chris Rogers
With thanks to the BBC National Orchestra of Wales
Original Theme Music: Ron Grainer
Casting Director: Andy Pryor CDG
Production Executive: Julie Scott
Production Accountant: Endaf Emyr Williams
Sound Recordist: Julian Howarth
    [uncredited: Ray Parker, Richard Dyer]
Costume Designer: Louise Page
Make-Up Designer Barbara Southcott
Music: Murray Gold
Visual Effects: The Mill
Visual FX Producers: Will Cohen, Marie Jones
Visual FX Supervisor: Dave Houghton
Prosthetics: Millennium FX
Special Effects: Any Effects
Editor: John Richards
Production Designer: Edward Thomas
Director of Photography: Rory Taylor
Production Manager: Tracie Simpson
    [uncredited: Debbi Slater]
Executive Producers: Russell T Davies,
    Julie Gardner
BBC Wales in association with the Canadian
Broadcasting Corporation
© MMVII

Profile

ANNA HOPE Novice Hame

Anna Hope reprised her role as the cat-like nurse nun in this episode, having first played Hame in *New Earth* [2006 – see Volume 51]. In fact Hope's first appearance as Hame had been in the brief *Tardisode* download made to publicise the episode, rendered in the style of an advert for the New New York Hospital.

Not only an actress but also more recently a fiction writer, Hope was born in 1974 and grew up in the village of Edgworth, Darwen in Lancashire, attending Edgworth Primary School and Turton High School before moving to Manchester with her family at 16. Her first experience of acting was putting on small plays at home with her sisters and she soon joined the local Octagon Youth Theatre in nearby Bolton, aged 10.

On leaving school, Hope studied English at Wadham College, Oxford, then attended RADA (where among other things she spent six weeks learning how to be an iguana), graduating in 2001, and later qualified with an MA in creative writing from Birkbeck College, London.

Hope auditioned for the part of Hame with 20 other actresses and although delighted to win the role, was immediately concerned that playing a cat-like being might demand complex feline choreography and gestures. In fact, make-up was all that was really needed to effect the transformation. As Hope recalled; "I was in make-up for three hours while they put the mask on and I had to have a new one made every day." Indeed the mask took another hour just to remove at the end of each day's filming. Recording *New Earth* took her 10 days on set, with *Gridlock* taking five.

The Hame who appeared in *New Earth* was kindly but misguided, tending to the Face of Boe while caught up in the 'flesh' scam perpetrated by the nuns of the Sisters of Plenitude. It is rehabilitated as Boe's carer that she returns in *Gridlock*, set 30 years after the events of *New Earth*.

Elsewhere in the *Doctor Who* universe, Hope has now starred in three *Doctor Who* audio dramas produced by Big Finish as Salford-based police detective DI Patricia Menzies, alongside Colin Baker's Sixth Doctor. Her three audios are *The Condemned* (2008), *The Raincloud Man* (2008) and *The Crimes of Thomas Brewster* (2011). Of the brash Menzies she says; "She doesn't take any nonsense from anybody... she has this whole kind

Right:
Novice Hame has atoned for her past crimes and is no longer a bad cat.

Below:
Cat fight!

of reality shift when she encounters the Doctor. She has to take on a whole new world." Hope had one problem recreating the role as she had recorded her début audio with a huskier voice while suffering from a cold.

Hope marked her writing début with her novel *Wake*, published in 2014 by Random House (and in paperback in 2015). The story of World War One seen through the eyes of three very different women and how it changed them, Hope was inspired by biographical accounts of turn of the century suffrage and growing women's rights. *The New York Times* commented: "Hope's unblinking prose is reminiscent of Vera Brittain's classic memoir *Testament of Youth*."

Hope's TV acting credits have included *Crime and Punishment* (2002), *The Long Firm* (2004), *Love Me Still* (2008), *Waking the Dead* (2011) and *Coronation Street* (2011-12). ■

DALEKS IN MANHATTAN/ EVOLUTION OF THE DALEKS

❯ STORY 182

New York. 1930. The Great Depression. Amidst the hardship and poverty, the Doctor and Martha unearth a sinister Dalek plot behind the construction of the Empire State Building.

Introduction

The cliffhanger at the end of *Daleks in Manhattan* – the first part of this double-length Dalek tale – must count as one of the most extraordinary moments in the history of *Doctor Who*. Having earlier swallowed up the unscrupulous Mr Diagoras, Dalek Sec's casing cracks open to reveal a monocular monster, decked out in the entrepreneur's pinstripe suit, wearing stubby tentacles like grisly dreadlocks. It's a hybrid creation made from Diagoras and the Dalek mutant.

It's not just a notable occasion for pure spectacle, however. This hybrid is the embodiment of an idea that is the ultimate perversion of what the Daleks represent: a Dalek who is embracing humanity.

As introduced in *The Mutants* [AKA *The Daleks*, 1963/4 – see Volume 1], the Daleks were created in opposition to our own ideals. It wasn't until the Second Doctor's era – by which time they'd gained quite a reputation for oppressing the human race – that the idea of a 'Human Dalek' arose. In *The Evil of the Daleks* [1967 – see Volume 10], Daleks are impregnated with the Human Factor – a distillation of the characteristics found in our race. In this instance, however, the Emperor Dalek's original plan was merely to identify the Human Factor so they could establish its negative image – the Dalek Factor – with which he intended to infect humanity throughout time.

This isn't what's going on in *Daleks in Manhattan/Evolution of the Daleks*. Introduced in *Army of Ghosts/Doomsday* [2006 – see Volume 53], the Cult of Skaro is a team of Daleks tasked with thinking outside their usual parameters. The original intention was that this team, led by Dalek Sec, would be an invaluable asset in assuring the Daleks' dominance over all other races. Backed into a corner, however, Sec comes to question Dalek philosophy. Could it be that humanity is more adaptable and therefore more successful? Could humans actually be better than the Daleks?

This presents the Doctor with a dilemma. Should he encourage this quantum leap in the evolution of this most reviled of species? Ultimately, it is a decision that is taken out of his hands... but a Dalek similar to the unprecedented, enlightened kind spawned in this story, will ultimately help him defeat Davros' apocalyptic designs when he meets him later in *The Stolen Earth/Journey's End* [2008 – see Volume 60]. ◾

Below: It all ends in tears for Dalek Sec.

'SHOULD THE DOCTOR ENCOURAGE THIS QUANTUM LEAP IN THE EVOLUTION OF THE DALEKS?'

STORY
Daleks in Manhattan

Tallulah is the star attraction of the New York Revue. She's visited in her dressing room by her boyfriend, Laszlo, who gives her a rose. After Tallulah has gone, Laszlo investigates an odd grunting coming from a storeroom – and is rushed by a man with a pig's head! [1]

The TARDIS materialises at the Statue of Liberty. Martha picks up a newspaper which gives the date – 1 November 1930 – and has the headline *Hooverville Mystery Deepens*.

The Doctor takes Martha to Hooverville, a shanty town in Central Park occupied by the unemployed and homeless led by a man called Solomon, who welcomes the Doctor. [2]

The Empire State Building is in the final stages of construction. Mr Diagoras orders the foreman to make his men work faster on behalf of his new masters – the Daleks! [3] The foreman is hauled away by pig slaves to be part of the Final Experiment.

Solomon confirms to the Doctor that men have been going missing from Hooverville. The camp is visited by Diagoras, looking for volunteers to help clear a collapsed sewer tunnel. The Doctor volunteers. Diagoras takes the Doctor, Martha, Solomon and a man called Frank down to the sewers and gives them directions. They head off and the Doctor discovers some strange, green, jellyfish-like matter. [4]

In the Empire State Building, Diagoras instructs the new foreman to fix some Dalek panels to the tower's mast. A Dalek joins Diagoras to gaze out across the city. [5] It observes that humankind survives while its own race has been destroyed. Diagoras is taken to the laboratory in the basement, where he is greeted by Dalek Sec before being grabbed by two pig slaves.

The Doctor, Martha, Solomon and Frank discover a pig slave squatting in the tunnels. [6] Then more pig slaves arrive and they are forced to flee, narrowly escaping by climbing a ladder to the theatre storeroom. Frank, however, isn't quick enough and is pulled down by the pig slaves. Then Tallulah enters, brandishing a gun. [7]

In her dressing room, she explains to the Doctor, Martha and Solomon that Laszlo disappeared two weeks ago. The Doctor agrees to help find him but first he has to analyse the jellyfish-like matter. Tallulah tells Martha that even though Laszlo has vanished, someone is leaving a rose for her every day.

That night, Solomon returns to Hooverville to tell the men to gather weapons. The Dalek panels are secured to the Empire State Building's mast. In the laboratory, Dalek Sec tells Dalek Thay that it intends to adapt to survive. It opens its casing, grabs Diagoras and drags him inside. [8]

While the Doctor analyses the jellyfish , Tallulah performs *My Angel Put the Devil in Me* on stage. [9] Martha spots a figure in the wings and gives chase. She is grabbed by a pig slave and taken into the sewers, where she is reunited with Frank.

The Doctor and Tallulah search for Martha in the sewers. They duck out of sight as a Dalek glides past, then discover a figure cowering in the darkness. It is Laszlo, who has been turned into a pig slave, but escaped before they converted his mind. He is reunited with a tearful Tallulah. [10]

Laszlo leads the Doctor and Tallulah to where the Daleks are selecting which of their prisoners will become pig slaves and which will be part of the Final Experiment. [11]

The Doctor joins Martha and Frank as they are led to the laboratory, where Sec is in "the final stage of evolution". Its casing opens and Diagoras emerges – but with a Dalek head. "I am a Human Dalek," it announces. "I am your future." [12]

Evolution of the Daleks

Sec orders the Daleks not to exterminate the Doctor and tells him that the Cult of Skaro came to 1930 using an emergency temporal shift. Sec feels everything it wanted from humanity; ambition, hatred, aggression and a genius for war. The Doctor uses his sonic screwdriver to disorientate the Daleks and escapes with Martha, Frank and Tallulah. [1]

The Daleks discuss Sec. After checking that no-one's listening, they admit they have doubts. [2]

Back at Hooverville, the Doctor warns Solomon that the Daleks will attack. But he's too late. Pig slaves scuttle through the camp and the Doctor and his friends are surrounded. A Dalek flies towards them. [3]

Solomon appeals to the Dalek's compassion, but it kills him. Incensed, the Doctor offers to let the Dalek exterminate him if it will spare the humans; it is about to do so when Sec commands it to stop. The Doctor is intrigued by the idea of a Dalek changing its mind and gives Martha his psychic paper before the Daleks escort him away.

Sec reveals the true extent of the Final Experiment to the Doctor. The Daleks have gathered over a thousand humans and wiped their minds, ready to be turned into a Human Dalek race. [4] Sec intends to use gamma radiation from an imminent solar flare to splice its DNA into the humans. It wants the Doctor to help make the new race more human.

Martha, Tallulah and Frank sneak into the Empire State Building using the psychic paper and ascend to the top floor. Examining the plans, Martha deduces that the Daleks have fixed Dalekanium to the mast! [5]

Laszlo enters the laboratory with the pig slaves. Sec informs the Doctor that the pig slaves only survive a few weeks. [6] The Doctor prepares a solution to

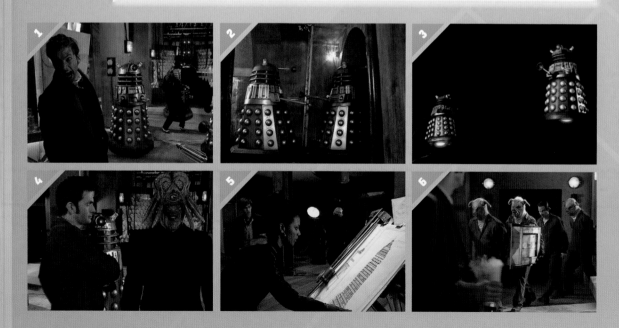

allow the gene bonds to reconfigure in a new pattern which is administered to the humans. But then the other Daleks enter and declare Sec their enemy.

The Doctor and Laszlo escape in the lift to the top floor, where the Doctor tells Martha that he has to remove the Dalekanium before the mast is struck by gamma radiation. The Doctor climbs on to the roof while Martha devises a plan to conduct lightning into the lift. The lift ascends, full of pig slaves. [7]

The Doctor drops the sonic screwdriver before removing the final Dalekanium panel. The lightning strikes and passes through the Doctor, clinging to the mast [8] before being conducted into the lift where it electrocutes the pig slaves. In the laboratory, the converted humans wake and are ordered by the Daleks to invade Manhattan.

Martha climbs on to the roof and returns the sonic screwdriver to the Doctor. He recovers and tells his friends that he must face the Dalek-controlled

humans in the theatre. Once they get there, the Doctor alerts the Daleks to his whereabouts and a group of Dalek-controlled humans march in, carrying Dalek weapons.

The Daleks appear on stage with Sec in chains. [9] They exterminate Sec and order the humans to kill the Doctor and his friends. But the humans received some Time Lord DNA when the Doctor got in the way of the lightning strike and they turn their fire against the Daleks. [10]

The remaining Dalek in the laboratory, Caan, has all the converted humans destroyed by remote control and escapes from the Doctor via an emergency temporal shift. [11]

Laszlo is brought in, close to death, but the Doctor manages to save his life. Later, Frank offers Laszlo a home in Hooverville. Laszlo still has the love of Tallulah and, leaving with the Doctor, Martha calls them "the pig and the showgirl". [12]

Pre-production

"New York, 1930s, Pig Men, sewers, showgirls, the Empire State Building – and Daleks," was Russell T Davies' 'shopping list' for the first two-part story of the 2007 series.

The person whose job it was to fit these requirements into a narrative was Helen Raynor, who had worked on *Doctor Who* as a script editor since the series returned to production in 2004. At the end of February 2006, Raynor had submitted her draft script of *Ghost Machine*, an episode of *Torchwood* (on which show she was also script editor on the episode *Greeks Bearing Gifts*). Although the idea of the Daleks in New York had originally been offered to Steven Moffat, he was too busy on the BBC One series *Jekyll* to write a two-part story. Thus it was decided that Helen would be assigned the first two-parter of the 2007 series of *Doctor Who*, and shortly afterwards she was invited into executive producer Julie Gardner's office where Russell T Davies presented her with his idea. "I think I stopped breathing – if he'd got down on one knee and proposed I couldn't have been more surprised," Helen told *Doctor Who Magazine*.

"I think you're mad, but please can I go home and think about it, because I'm still slightly in shock," Helen told Julie and Russell. Considering the offer that night, she quickly emailed to accept the opportunity. Julie Gardner offered Helen a sabbatical from her script editor's post to write the episodes, but the writer refused, preferring instead to drop down to two days a week on *Doctor Who* and remain working on a new script being developed by Steven Moffat, with whom she had worked closely since *The Empty Child* [2005 – see Volume 50] in 2004. A new script editor joined the team in the form of Lindsey Alford, who had been working on the BBC One medical drama *Casualty*. By the end of March, the story was in the schedule and, in April, further discussions with Davies had helped in the development of the storyline to incorporate the requested elements.

Into the past

There was to be a twist in the setting for the new Dalek story in comparison to stories such as *Dalek* [2005 – see Volume 49], *Bad Wolf/The Parting of the Ways* [2005 – see Volume 50] and *Army of Ghosts/Doomsday* [2006 – see Volume 53]. "We've had Daleks in the far future, we've had them in the present day, so a new setting to revitalise them is the past," said Russell in *Doctor Who Confidential*, adding, with reference to serials like *The Chase* [1965 – see Volume 5] and *The Evil of the Daleks* [1967 – see Volume 10], "It was always a nice image – Daleks in the past."

The historical setting is the stylish Art Deco New York of the 1930s and the Art Deco Empire State Building, the 102-storey skyscraper designed by William F Lamb and Gregory Johnson which was begun in March 1930 and officially opened in May 1931, with its topmost antenna – added in March 1931 – almost 1,500 feet off the ground. The building had been seen briefly when the TARDIS and a pursuing Dalek time

'THE HISTORICAL SETTING IS THE STYLISH ART DECO NEW YORK OF THE 1930S.'

Above:
The pig-headed servants of the Daleks.

machine arrived there in *Flight Through Eternity*, the third episode of *The Chase*. "I like to think that when they landed there, the Dalek memory banks made a little record of the building," said Russell T Davies in *Doctor Who Confidential*, adding, "All I said to Helen was 1930's New York. I knew the Empire State Building existed in the 1930s, but it was her idea to actually make the construction of it part of the story."

The inclusion of the Pig Men continued the tradition of the Daleks using mindless humanoid servants such as the Robomen in 1964's *The Dalek Invasion of Earth* [see Volume 4] and the Ogrons introduced in 1972's *Day of the Daleks* [see Volume 17]. Davies saw the Pig Men as a fun element, and at an early stage they were to have been created from pigs and sailors, snatched from the New York Docks, which the writer believed could be recorded at Cardiff Docks. In *Radio Times* he explained,

Connections: Sonnet

⟩ On seeing the Statue of Liberty, the Doctor quotes: "Give me your tired, your poor, your huddled masses yearning to breathe free," from Emma Lazarus' 1883 sonnet *The New Colossus* which was inscribed inside the Statue of Liberty in 1903.

"The key to it all, where the whole Pig Men thing comes from, and the *Island of Dr Moreau* feel to it, is that Daleks were born out of a genetic experiment, and that makes them great geneticists... It was time to put the Daleks back where they really belong, in that sphere." As well as tapping into current fears about stem cell research, Davies was drawing upon HG Wells' 1896 novel in which Dr Moreau transformed beasts into man-like creatures.

"I was very influenced by horror films of the time, especially *Frankenstein*... so creepy sewers, showgirls in peril, and lab experiments all fell into my lap," Helen Raynor told *Doctor Who Magazine*. Mary Shelley's 1818 novel of how a surgeon brought to life a body assembled from cadavers with energy conducted from a lightning strike had formed the basis of Universal Pictures' 1931 movie, and this was echoed by the activation of the Dalek Hybrids from the gamma energy hitting the mast atop the Empire State Building. This mast, which had fascinated the press while the iconic building was under construction, also captured Raynor's imagination.

It's showtime!

Setting the story in the Depression following the Wall Street Crash during the presidency of Herbert Hoover from March 1929, the writer saw the story as very brutal, showing people as an expendable commodity. The first image of New York during the Depression that Helen Raynor and Russell T Davies had in mind was that of brownstone tenement buildings, which did not make its way into the final script. "It's hard to do 1930s New York in Cardiff, let's be honest," admitted Davies on *Doctor Who Confidential*, and so the venues for the story were chosen very carefully to limit exterior work to what could be effectively achieved.

"I knew from the start that street scenes were going to be horrendously expensive and difficult to realise, so I concentrated on getting the most out of locations that were key to the story," said Helen Raynor in *Doctor Who Magazine*. The main exterior to be used would be that of Central Park, the location of a Hooverville, the nickname given to Depression shanty towns across the USA where the unemployed and homeless dwelt. One of these actually existed in Central Park in an area where the Lower Reservoir was being landscaped between 1931 and 1933; Raynor seized on this and the production team agreed it was an ideal setting for the story. In sharp contrast to the poverty of Hooverville, the glamour and glitz of Manhattan was to be shown in other ways. Recalling the climax of the 1933 monster movie *King Kong,* Russell T Davies suggested the inclusion of a theatre with showgirls. "It was actually quite a grim story and to get some colour and fun in there, a theatre was a fantastic setting," explained Raynor in *Doctor Who Confidential*. Having

worked in the theatre, the writer knew she could draw upon her knowledge of the backstage atmosphere, and also create a heart-warming and hopeful love story for the characters of the singer Tallulah – named after the speakeasy singer in the 1976 children's gangster musical *Bugsy Malone* – and the stagehand Laszlo (specified as Polish in earlier drafts of the script) who was transformed into a Pig Man by the Daleks. *"The Phantom of the Opera* was a big influence... what you need is a monster with a good heart," commented Raynor in *Radio Times*, referring to the Gaston Laroux story originally serialised in 1909-1910 which tells of a disfigured musical genius beneath the Opera Garnier in Paris and his obsession with a beautiful singer.

On writing a Dalek story, Helen Raynor told *Totally Doctor Who*, "It was really strange, because I can remember them

Connections: The Cult

▸ The Doctor had first encountered the four Daleks that make up the Cult of Skaro - Dalek Sec, Dalek Caan, Dalek Thay and Dalek Jast - in *Army of Ghosts/Doomsday* [2006 - see Volume 53]. There they escaped being thrown back into the void by initiating an emergency temporal shift - presumably transporting them to New York in the early twentieth century.

Below: Martha makes her Broadway début!

"THE DALEKS HAVE
TO BE INCREDIBLY
INTELLIGENT."

so clearly from when I was a kid and how scary they were." The writer watched various Dalek serials from the 80s and realised that the creatures were driven by ambition and survival; they had also been created by genetic experimentation which pointed the way ahead for their species to evolve, allowing the creation of the Dalek Sec Hybrid as a prophet/orator figure. "Russell T Davies' main advice was that the Daleks have to be incredibly intelligent," she told *Doctor Who Magazine*. "The minute that you diminish them as an enemy, you diminish the Doctor's fight against them." Mr Diagoras – named after a fifth-century BC Greek poet – was originally more of a classic "moustachioed villain" while the writer saw Solomon as an inspiring father figure, with both men having lived through similar experiences in the Great War, but having been changed by them in very different ways.

Flight to New York

"I wrote some wildly over-ambitious stuff in the first drafts," Raynor told *Doctor Who Magazine*. At the end of June, Julie and Russell were very positive about the state of *Daleks in Manhattan*, of which the writer explained in *Radio Times*, "The first draft had Tallulah stumbling on to the caged survivors of the early Dalek experiments." This sequence – with every creature needing to be a different design – was deemed too expensive. In this early version, the TARDIS arrived on a Broadway rooftop in Times Square which allowed the Doctor and Martha to look out across Manhattan ... but was deemed too expensive.

Other ideas discussed in early versions of the scripts included that the Pig Men should be dressed in 1930's suits (dropped so as not to look too much like *The Wind in*

the Willows), a steam-driven Dalek patched up with wood following its arrival in New York (abandoned as it detracted from the Hybrid storyline), tentacles emerging from Dalek Sec to drag Diagoras inside, a more elaborate musical set piece featuring lobsters and shrimps plus Baroque cut-out waves, Laszlo's connections with New York's criminal underworld, and plans to feature drinking dens and speakeasies of the Prohibition Era (dropped because Russell T Davies disliked any location where jazz music might be played!). The dock setting was dropped as it was deemed to be complicated in terms of geography relative to the theatre and the sewers; this meant that the idea of lighting moving underwater – indicating Daleks – was also dropped, and that the initial idea of the Doctor investigating the theft of pigs at the docks was omitted. With *Daleks in Manhattan* completed, Raynor's task for *Evolution of the Daleks* was to take all the elements previously established and turn them into a conclusive narrative. This was easier said than done. "I did the classic writer thing of realising that there were things in the story that just didn't work – you can set them up, but you can't make them pay off," the writer explained

Below: Mr Diagoras looks for new recruits.

DALEKS IN MANHATTAN / EVOLUTION OF THE DALEKS STORY 182

Above:
Three
members of
the Cult
of Skaro.

in *Doctor Who Magazine*. The first draft of this concluding instalment was discussed with Russell, Julie, Lindsey and the second incoming script editor, Gary Russell (a long-standing *Doctor Who* novelist, former editor of *Doctor Who Magazine* and producer of *Doctor Who* audio plays for Big Finish). The discussions helped shape the episode in subsequent drafts, but during the process Helen still struggled with the ending, commenting, "I woke up at four in the morning very anxious. I didn't know how to solve the problem I was wrestling with."

On Thursday 17 August, James Strong found an answerphone message from producer Phil Collinson offering him the opportunity to direct a two-part Dalek story. Strong had previously directed the two-part *The Impossible Planet/The Satan*

Pit [2006 – see Volume 53] in February and March 2006, and was then in post-production for his two episodes of *Torchwood* – *Cyberwoman* and *They Keep Killing Suzie* – which comprised the third recording block of the series. Strong also came in to direct a unit to pick up some deferred scenes on *Smith and Jones* [2007 – see Volume 54] on Friday 25 August.

On Wednesday 30 August, Strong met Gillane Seaborne, the series producer of *Doctor Who Confidential*, who mentioned that she was planning to take Helen Raynor to New York to interview her in the setting for her story. Having been unhappy with the notion of relying on library footage of New York which might have been filmed at unsuitable angles or times of day, Strong decided to suggest to Collinson that a skeleton crew from the

Doctor Who team should also fly to New York to shoot background plate material of the city itself. The director was keen to give the episodes a distinctly different feel to his last *Doctor Who* story and looked at numerous films of the period, including Busby Berkeley musicals and photographs of the time, from which he drew on the iconic photograph *Lunch atop a Skyscraper* taken on 20 September 1932 which depicts workers sitting on girders high above the city as they build the Rockefeller Center; such images had also inspired Helen Raynor. "It was a challenge to make [the episodes] just as cinematic and exciting, but without having to rely on spooky corridors, and monsters," she told *Doctor Who Magazine*.

Location search

I n preparation for the story, Strong watched DVDs of several previous Dalek adventures. The script of *Daleks in Manhattan* was available on Saturday 16 September. On Monday 18, Collinson agreed to Strong's proposal for a New York shoot; a minimal crew would travel to the city with the *Doctor Who Confidential* team organising the visit. In the wake of 9/11, the city was very security-conscious and various special permissions had to be granted for recording there. While this was the show's first official recording in the USA, *Doctor Who* had filmed overseas in the past, travelling to Paris in 1979 for *City of Death* [1979 – see Volume 31], Amsterdam in 1982 for *Arc of Infinity* [1983 – see Volume 36], Lanzarote in 1983 for *Planet of Fire* [1984 – see Volume 39] and Seville in 1984 for *The Two Doctors* [1985 – see Volume 41], while the 1996 TV Movie [see Volume 47] had been a co-production made in Vancouver, Canada.

The script for *Evolution of the Daleks* arrived with Strong on Tuesday 19 September, a few days before the tone meeting for the two Dalek episodes, which formed the fourth recording block, was held on the morning of Friday 22 September. Strong was still in a state of euphoria from the birth of his son the previous morning, while Russell T Davies was unwell and unable to attend the discussion. One particular effect which was debated was the opening of Dalek Sec and its absorption of Diagoras, with Dave Houghton of The Mill suggesting the effect of tentacles created in CGI, akin to the face-hugger creature seen in the 1979 sci-fi thriller *Alien*.

On Tuesday 3 October, a preliminary search for locations led Strong to a perfect site for Hooverville in Cardiff. However, four days later, the city council informed Strong that his favoured venue was unavailable because it was a breeding ground for the rare great crested newt and could not be disturbed by the BBC crew.

Connections: Catchphrase

❯ In *Evolution of the Daleks,* the Doctor uses one of his favourite phrases – "Allons-y!" – which he had previously toyed with in *Army of Ghosts/Doomsday* [2006 – see Volume 53].

Below: The Doctor is powerless to help when the Daleks attack Hooverville.

DALEKS IN MANHATTAN / EVOLUTION OF THE DALEKS

The main casting session took place in London on Sunday 8 October, and for many of the roles Strong aimed to cast American actors to get authentic accents; these included Andrew Garfield who had played Tom in *Sugar Rush,* Joe Montana who had been a commander in the 2005 episode *Dalek* [see Volume 49] and Eric Loren, cast as Mr Diagoras, who had played a Cyclops in the 1990 film *Nightbreed*. The director had previously worked with Hugh Quarshie on *Holby City,* where Quarshie played Ric Griffin. Miranda Raison had played Jo Portman in *Spooks* and for her role as Tallulah would get tuition on her accent from an American voice coach. The role of Laszlo went to American actor Ryan Carnes, who was best known for his appearances in *Desperate Housewives*. The actor was represented in the UK by the same agent as Captain Jack actor John Barrowman, and he had arranged a meeting between Ryan Carnes and Julie Gardner to discuss the prospect of work in this country; the agent was also a fan of *Doctor Who*. Ironically, Carnes had grown up with pigs and was state champion for pig calling when he was 10 years old. "Playing a pig after working on a pig farm in the world capital of pigs [Pike County, Illinois] is all very strange," Carnes commented in the *Daily Record*.

Following revisions, a new version of the script was ready for the readthrough at the Holland House Hotel at 2.30pm on Monday 16 October. Following this initial reading – with senior brand executive Edward Russell standing in to perform the Dalek voices with a commercially available Dalek voice changer toy as Nicholas Briggs was unable to attend – David Tennant and Freema Agyeman departed to continue recording *The Lazarus Experiment*.

Right:
The Doctor is unable to return Laszlo to human form.

Left:
Solomon
breaks the
bread.

Below:
The Doctor
listens to Sec's
insane plan.

One of the main changes to the script was that Laszlo's life was now saved by the Doctor; originally he died looking up at Tallulah, commenting how she looked like an angel because of the tiara and winged costume worn in her song routine. "He has Russell T Davies to thank for his survival," Helen Raynor commented in the book *Doctor Who: Creatures and Demons*. "I originally killed him off in a scene of indulgent, heartrending tragedy, which didn't sit well in our optimistic series. It would have been a right downer for kids at Saturday teatime."

Baby alligators

The shooting scripts for *Daleks in Manhattan/Evolution of the Daleks* were issued on Monday 16 October. At the Laurenzi Theatre, the chorus girls were described as 'tough cookies with accents to match', Tallulah was described as '20s, sweet faced' while Laszlo was '20s, handsome and shy'. When the shadow flitted past Tallulah's dressing room door, it was referred to as 'very *Sixth Sense*' in reference to the 1999 paranormal film.

The TARDIS landed at the base of the Statue of Liberty. The Doctor correctly commented that New York was originally called New Amsterdam when it was a seventeenth-century Dutch colonial town. Originally, the newspaper on which Martha read the date of 1 November 1930 was blown in front of the TARDIS by the wind. The Doctor explained to Martha about Herbert Hoover, the President of the USA from March 1929 to March 1933, and the economic problems which had led to the creation of Hooverville.

Solomon was 'late 30s, black, authoritative' and originally the Doctor shook his hand on meeting him; the roots of his biblical name in the wise ruler of Israel were emphasized with him splitting a loaf of bread in half just as his namesake solved a quarrel over ownership of a baby by threatening to cut the infant in two. In the sewers, Martha referred to the urban myth of New Yorkers flushing baby alligators down the toilet [see *Gridlock*, page 15], and when examining the 'sinister jellyfish' in the sewers, the Doctor noted "radial nerve structure". When Diagoras gave the equipment for the mast to the workers, the stage directions noted, the metal plates were 'panels from a Dalek skirt'. The Transgenic Lab was described as 'an 'industrial' Dalek laboratory; a mix of Dalek 'design' and genuine 1930s

Connections:
Unlikely couple

▶ Martha's description of Laszlo and Tallulah as "the pig and the showgirl" is a play on the 1957 romantic comedy movie *The Prince and the Showgirl*.

equipment. Flasks bubble, flames leap, it's all very active.'

Working in the theatre basement, the Doctor used 'a Hamilton Colt radio (1930's portable)' found by Solomon. For the actual performance, the dance number was described as 'lyrics TBA'.

Of the climax to *Daleks in Manhattan*, Helen Raynor commented on *Totally Doctor Who*, "I wanted to write a cliffhanger where everybody was in a huge amount of danger, a huge amount of trouble, and you've got no idea how they're going to get out." The humanoid form which stepped from the Dalek casing was 'recognisable as being Mr Diagoras... but where the head should be, there's a familiar squid-like whitish glob – with a single eye, and tentacles stretching, Medusa-like, around it. The human mouth visible, moving when he speaks.'

In *Evolution of the Daleks*, Solomon's original speech to the Daleks about God included him saying, "If His different creations can't find some connection, then what hope is there? For any of us?" When the Hybrids in the Transgenic Lab were revealed, the script noted, 'Hanging down from the ceiling on wires are hundreds of stretchers, on different levels, like in [the 1978 suspense movie] *Coma*. Nearly all of the stretchers are occupied by white body bags (we can't see what's inside).' One of the body bags, 'falls open easily, not like a modern SOC [Scene Of Crime] body bag.' Inside was a 'Human Body. Very pale, androgynous, wearing something like a 1930s suit or tunic.'

Reaching the summit of the Empire State Building, Tallulah quoted Jimmy Cagney from the 1949 movie *White Heat*: 'Top of the world!' Martha spoke of meeting the Doctor in a hospital in *Smith and Jones* and there were oblique references to Rose. The weapons used by the Dalek-Humans were described as 'Dalek guns, adapted into machine-gun form'. The Daleks featured were members of the Cult of Skaro seen in *Doomsday*, and the Daleks referred to the war which destroyed their home planet Skaro. There were references to the creation of the Daleks as seen in the 1975 serial *Genesis of the Daleks* [see Volume 23] where the scientist Davros had designed the Daleks as a means for the survival of the Kaled race on Skaro. The Daleks also measured time in 'rels', originally defined as a unit of hydroelectricity in 1964's *The*

Right:
Sec is deemed irrelevant by the rest of the Cult of Skaro.

Above:
"Come on! Give
us a song!"

Dalek Book, as in *Doomsday* and the 1966 movie *Dalek's Invasion Earth 2150 AD*.

The pre-credits took place on 'Night A', with the main narrative opening in the TARDIS on 'Night 5' before the ship's arrival in New York on 'Day 6'. The climax of the story then occurred on 'Night 6' before the TARDIS departed on the morning of 'Day 6A'.

Porcine prosthetics

On Tuesday 17 October, Strong received a tape of the basic dance routine from choreographer Ailsa Berk. At this point, the number was choreographed to *Anything Goes* by Cole Porter. However it was soon realised that this had been written in 1934 so they recorded the song – *My Angel Put the Devil in Me* (also known as *Heaven and Hell*) by Murray Gold the following week. Miranda Raison had a little extra dancing tuition and recorded the vocals for the song herself.

Pink amendments were made on Tuesday 17 covering the start of the pre-credits, the Doctor and Martha making for Hooverville, the appearance of Solomon to the first appearance of the bronze Dalek, Diagoras talking to the workers, Diagoras and the bronze Dalek looking out across Manhattan, the Doctor's party encountering something in the sewer, the group being pursued by the Pig Men to their meeting with Tallulah, the workers toiling on the mast, the start of the performance at the theatre, the Doctor and Tallulah seeing Daleks in the sewers, Martha and Frank being herded along with the other prisoners, and the selected prisoners being taken to the Transgenic Laboratory.

For *Evolution of the Daleks*, pink amendments made on Wednesday 18 covered from the Doctor talking to the Hybrid Sec through to the party's return

to Hooverville, the Doctor discussing the Hybrids and the flare with Sec, Martha talking to Tallulah about being a doctor, the overriding of the gene feed, the Doctor working at the mast, the Dalek linking into the battle computer, the Doctor confronting the Daleks at the theatre, and then the defeat of the Daleks to the end of the story.

Technical recces were held for the episodes on Wednesday 18 and Thursday 19, followed by a production meeting at Upper Boat; on the second of these days, Dave Houghton spotted a wall opposite Penarth Leisure Centre which would be ideal for the base of the Statue of Liberty. In tandem with work on various other episodes on Thursday 19 October, Ruari Mears, who was playing a Gold Head Robot on pick-ups of *The Runaway Bride* [2006 – see Volume 54], donned Millennium FX's Pig Man make-up for the team's 'show and tell' session of the porcine prosthetics before changing outfits for his robotic role. While the team were delighted with the foam latex pig mask, it was felt that the ears were too perky and friendly, so these were later crumpled and bent over to make the Hybrids more menacing. ∎

Connections: Second time around

> Martha made reference to New New York, which she had visited in *Gridlock* [see page 6]. The Doctor then commented, "So good they named it twice," in reference to the song *New York, New York*, the theme song to the 1977 movie of the same name.

Production

From Tuesday 10 to Thursday 12 October, teams from *Doctor Who Confidential* and *Doctor Who* flew to New York. The *Doctor Who* team comprised James Strong, Phil Collinson, Dave Houghton and a cameraman only. Setting out at 5am the next morning, the crew beat the tourists up the Empire State Building on Fifth Avenue to record various plate shots under different lighting conditions looking out across the metropolis from the freezing observation gallery on the 86th floor. Saturday 14 October saw the crew travel to Liberty Island at the mouth of New York Harbor to record establishing shots of the Statue of Liberty and also distant shots of the Empire State Building across the bay. That afternoon, the team returned to Fifth Avenue where a rooftop bar gave them the angles they

"NOT ONLY COULD I NOT SEE,
IT WAS ALSO HARD TO HEAR WHAT
DAVID TENNANT WAS SAYING."

Connections:
The Last Great
Time War

▶ Martha recognised the
name of the Daleks as the
Doctor had told her about
how his own people had
battled them at the
end of *Gridlock*
[see page 6].

wanted looking up at the Empire State. The team's final day in New York, Sunday 15, began with an establishing shot of the Majestic Theatre – appropriately home to the record-breaking musical *The Phantom of the Opera* – a 1927 building on 44th Street, and then travelled to Manhattan's famous Central Park for shots of the park's skyline with the Empire State again firmly in evidence. In particular, the crew wanted to get reference shots of 1930s period buildings.

Following on from production of *The Lazarus Experiment*, recording on Episodes 4 and 5 began on Monday 23 October at Upper Boat studios, where Mr Diagoras' office high in the partially completed Empire State Building had been constructed, with large fans creating the effect of strong winds at such a great height and a greenscreen for the vista outside to be added in post-production. David Tennant and Freema Agyeman were not required for the first day's recording,

which focused on scenes for *Daleks in Manhattan*, with *Doctor Who Confidential* present to capture Helen Raynor's first sight of her story in production. Recording ran a standard 8am to 7pm, although Barnaby Edwards, who was operating Bronze Dalek #1 or Dalek Caan – a task he had undertaken since *Dalek* in 2004 – was needed for a practice session from 7am, and Nicholas Briggs was on hand with his ring modulator voice box to provide the electronic voice. For this serial, Briggs voiced Dalek Thay in the manner of former Dalek voice artiste Roy Skelton, made Caan's voice higher than before, pitched Jast very high and spoke in a normal tone for Sec. The radio-controlled elements of the Daleks were again operated by Colin Newman. Paul Kasey played the main Pig Man, with Rob Mayor and Pete Hawkins of Millennium Effects supervising the application of the prosthetics. The scene of Diagoras and the Dalek looking out across Manhattan caused problems as Edwards had difficulty in getting his Dalek casing to move steadily over the slightly uneven floor.

David and Freema joined the crew for work on Tuesday 24 where more of the office scenes were completed, while Ailsa Berk was rehearsing the Pig Men performers in front of the TARDIS set nearby from 9.30am. This was also the first day that Carnes underwent his three-hour prosthetic application as the foam latex porcine version of Laszlo crafted by Rob Mayor and applied by Sarah Lockwood. "I watched a couple of episodes [of *Doctor Who*] before I came over to the UK and I thought to myself, 'How are the Daleks that scary?'" Carnes told the *Daily Record*. "Then I got on set and one of them rolled out behind me and I got a real fright." When Edwards was needed in London to record a BBC Digital trailer, Nicholas Pegg

Below:
Dalek voice
artist, Nicholas
Briggs (far left),
with the Dalek
operators
and crew.

– another veteran Dalek operator – stood in for him as Caan. The same set was used the next day with a second camera in use for scenes from *Evolution of the Daleks*, after which the TARDIS sequence at the start of *Daleks in Manhattan* was recorded. David and Freema also recorded special links on the TARDIS set for *Children in Need,* which would be the first appearance of the pair on screen in costume for the series.

Down the drain

Blue script amendments on Wednesday 25 October covered Tallulah talking to Martha in the dressing room, the Daleks debating the Final Experiment, Martha seeing the Pig Laszlo in the wings, and the very end of *Daleks in Manhattan*. Similar changes to *Evolution of the Daleks* covered from the attack on Hooverville to Solomon addressing the Daleks, from Solomon's

death to Sec's admission that the deaths were wrong, Sec explaining about the solar flare, the scene in the work lift, and Martha searching the office and her plan to "zap" the lift. On the eve of her first day with the Daleks, Freema received a text message from Russell T Davies: 'Martha meets the Daleks. You've arrived!'

Taping on the office set was concluded on Thursday 26 October along with the scenes in the lift (with Barnaby Edwards effectively hired to sit motionless in a Dalek casing in all these elevator sequences), and following this work began on sequences in the New York sewers with the Doctor and Tallulah. The crew had briefly considered recording the sewer sequences on location, but found that the health and safety implications outweighed the cost of constructing a set. A horseshoe-shaped section of subterranean passage was constructed at Upper Boat which could be re-dressed and recorded from

Connections:
Return visit

▶ The Daleks had previously visited the Empire State Building when their own time ship landed there in *Flight Through Eternity*, the third episode of *The Chase* [1965 – see Volume 5]. On that occasion, a single Dalek briefly explored the public observation deck and encountered tourist Morton Dill.

different angles to represent six sewer segments; Any Effects provided the dank, dripping atmosphere for this setting. Joining the team as Dalek Jast or 'Bronze Enemy #3' (as the Daleks were now referred to on the call sheets in an attempt to keep their return to the series under wraps) was David Hankinson, who had been a Dalek operator since *Bad Wolf* in early 2005. David chatted to David Tennant for his BBC Worldwide video diary during the day and Miranda also spoke on camera to the show's star.

The scenes with the Doctor and Tallulah for *Daleks in Manhattan* were completed with other sewer scenes on Friday 27 October, with Millennium FX providing the 'Enemy Remains' glob studied by the Doctor.

Yellow script amendments were issued on the same day. These covered the Doctor's first meeting with Solomon, Mr Diagoras drumming up a labour group in Hooverville, Martha talking to Frank in the sewers, the Doctor talking to the Pig Man in the sewers and the Doctor probing the Dalek glob at the theatre (which had originally been written to take place in the gods, but needed transferring away due to the crew's limited time at the theatre).

At Upper Boat, sewer work continued on Saturday 28 October with sequences for both episodes, and stunt arranger Tom Lucy supervising the *Daleks in Manhattan* scene where the Pig Men grabbed Frank during the escape up the ladder. These sequences were continued on Monday 30 October, with Nicholas Pegg joining the cast to operate one of the Bronze Enemies – Dalek Thay, who was missing his rear

panels – required in the sewers. Elsewhere at Upper Boat, Ailsa Berk was rehearsing the movement of the 'Human Enemy' Hybrids from 9.45am, and a second unit was at work performing various inserts. Tom Lucy supervised the shots of the workmen sitting on the girder suspended before a greenscreen, after which more greenscreen was performed for passers-by outside the theatre. Other insert shots showed a Dalek eye close-up in the office and the green glob in the sewers, with *Doctor Who Confidential* following this effects work. After wrap at 7pm, David Tennant stayed on for a special unit photoshoot of him as the Doctor. Meanwhile at Millennium FX in Chesham that morning, Eric Loren had his final prosthetic fitting for his role of 'Black Human Enemy' which had been crafted on a cast of his head and was fitted by Pete Hawkins and Matt O'Toole with animatronics from Gustav Hoegen; the single eye for this mask was made to look more human than on the mutant seen in *Dalek*, and was blue to match the blue light on the Dalek eye stalks.

Tuesday 31 October saw the crew returning to the old NEG glass site at Trident Park in Cardiff Bay, a disused chemical works which offered a pillared

Right:
The Doctor decided he wasn't that hungry after all.

Above:
"I am Dalek in human form!"

vault that was perfect for the Transgenic Laboratory. "It was the coldest place I've ever filmed. It was like a tomb in there," recalled James Strong on the DVD episode commentary. All four 'Enemies' seen in *Doomsday* were now required, with Anthony Spargo – who had previously deputised for Edwards – as the 'Black Enemy' or Dalek Sec. A syringe was attached to Dalek Caan's arm for the injection scene in *Daleks in Manhattan*. It was also discovered that the hands for the human version of Sec had apparently not been budgeted for, and so a pair of black gloves were hurriedly added to Mr Diagoras' attire for his pre-transformation scenes. It was later found that the hands had, in fact, been ordered after all, and were used on the Dalek Sec Hybrid as planned. The gloves remained in the earlier Diagoras scenes as re-shoots would have been too costly.

Dalek delivery

Recording on Wednesday 1 November was scheduled slightly later from 9am to 8pm, with the scheduling of scenes with David and Freema later in the day, which generally covered the climactic transformation of Dalek Sec and scenes spanning both episodes. This was Eric Loren's first day in his Dalek Sec prosthetic. He was barely able to see and deafened by motors whirring in his headpiece. "I had this battery-operated sound in my ears... so not only could I not see, it was also hard to hear what David [Tennant] was saying. But we worked things out in rehearsals – he was fantastic," Loren told *Radio Times*. In fact, the prosthetic caused problems with camera angles and lighting for the team which the director had to battle with. To ensure that his Hybrid dialogue sounded authentically like a Dalek, Eric Loren had asked Nicholas Briggs to perform all his post-transformation dialogue without his ring modulator so that he could study Dalek delivery, and had also studied the voice of Davros on the DVD of *Genesis of the Daleks*. Eric and Ryan both spoke to David Tennant for his video diary during recordings. For the transformation scene, the Dalek prop was shaken from behind by props man Phil Shellard and filled with smoke by Any Effects, while Spargo wore a gas mask inside. Loren climbing out of the Dalek casing was recorded using a box on a greenscreen set, later matted on to the casing. On set, the music heard from the radio at the start of the second episode was originally *Barwick Green*, the maypole dance music from the 1924 suite *My Native Heath* written by Arthur Wood... and best-known as the theme tune to the BBC radio soap *The Archers*.

At the same time, Ailsa Berk rehearsed the professional dancers plus Miranda Raison, Flik Swan and Alexis Caley for the production number in London (attended by *Doctor Who Confidential*), and work continued at the NEG site

Connections: Stage fright

❯ When Tallulah asks Martha if she's ever been on stage before, Martha says she has had a little experience and mentions Shakespeare. This is a reference to the events of the earlier story, *The Shakespeare Code* [2007 – see Volume 54], in which Martha met the great bard.

Above:
Slave to the
Daleks!

on Thursday 2 November with the location owners visiting to see the strange goings on in their premises. Meanwhile, a second unit recorded close-up shots of liquid flowing to the lifeless Dalek Hybrids.

Freema was not needed for recording at the Transgenic Lab on Friday 3 where scenes from *Evolution of the Daleks* were enacted and Any Effects provided the requirements of flames and coloured liquid running through tubes (which were recorded in reverse). Visiting the set were Clayton Hickman and Tom Spilsbury from *Doctor Who Magazine*, and Lee Binding on behalf of the BBC's *Doctor Who* website.

Work continued for *Doctor Who* at the NEG glass site on Monday 6 with Transgenic Lab scenes for *Evolution of the Daleks* and a visual effects shot of Mr Diagoras for *Daleks in Manhattan*.

The final day on the lab set, Tuesday 7, focused on scenes for *Evolution of the Daleks* which required only the Hybrid Sec, the Daleks and the Pig Men, releasing David Tennant and Freema Agyeman who were needed to record inserts for other episodes in the series. Various effects shots were also performed for The Mill for the scenes where the Hybrids were energised and also for the shots on the Daleks' screen.

Back at Upper Boat on Wednesday 8, the sequences of the Doctor and Martha with the Dalek prisoners were recorded on the sewer set for *Daleks in Manhattan*. Johnny Davis of *GQ* Magazine visited the set to interview the series' two stars, while Claire Jones was also present to acquire material for the BBC's *Doctor Who* website in conjunction with *Doctor Who Confidential*.

Following the TARDIS exterior scenes and greenscreen work for the background shots of the harbour, the crew relocated to Blackweir Park close to where Hooverville was being constructed in the woodlands of Bute Park near Cardiff University. The area of Bute Park behind Cardiff Castle doubled for Central Park for the closing scene of Laszlo going to live in Hooverville and the *Daleks in Manhattan* sequence of the Doctor and Martha walking in the park. A sequence in Solomon's tent for *Evolution of the Daleks* was also recorded.

Poor weather

Doctor Who Confidential joined the crew on Thursday 9 November for recording at the Penarth Leisure Centre behind a primary school in Penarth where the wall matching the base of the Statue of Liberty had been found... and where the appearance of an iconic police box soon attracted the attention of eager young viewers! Two units were operating from 7.30am, with a morning of fine weather after two weeks of rain matching perfectly the plate shots of the statue recorded in October. While Phil Collinson was interviewed by the *Doctor Who Confidential* team about the New York shoot, David Tennant playfully complained that he didn't get to go to America at all and had to stay in Cardiff, adding, "And a local dog just weed on the TARDIS!"

"I WILL SACRIFICE MYSELF
FOR THE GREATER CAUSE,
THE FUTURE OF DALEK KIND."

Right:
The Doctor and Martha listen to Mr Diagoras offer work to the homeless of Hooverville.

Work with numerous extras started on the Hooverville set in earnest on Friday 10, with David Tennant commenting of the setting on *Doctor Who Confidential*, "It felt fantastically real because it existed on every side of you." The daytime scenes for *Daleks in Manhattan* were scheduled, with Tom Lucy supervising the fight over the bread between the two men. A second camera was at work, but the establishing shot of Hooverville had to be done several times when the name on its sign was misspelt.

Poor weather meant that the crew was behind schedule and the Hooverville scenes from Friday 10 were completed on the afternoon of Saturday 11. Armourer Faujja Singh joined the crew to supervise the use of firearms for the night-time scenes for the siege in *Evolution of the Daleks* with

recording going on to 11pm. *Doctor Who Confidential* was again on hand to see the major location shoot in progress.

The attack on Hooverville was recorded at Bute Park from 4pm to 3am on Monday 13 November, with Crispin Layfield supervising the stunt work performed by Kim McGarrity, Guy List and Andy Smart; these were largely leaps from hidden mini-trampettes as people were blown by the force of the explosions. Only four explosions were detonated, each covered by three cameras so they could appear from various angles. The positions of the hovering Daleks were indicated by cardboard cut-outs on long poles held by third assistant director Sarah Davies, and *Doctor Who Confidential* was again present.

On the afternoon of Tuesday 14 November, James Strong and Ailsa Berk supervised a dance rehearsal at the Park & Dare Theatre in Treorchy. This was a miners' theatre built in 1913 which had

Connections: Space metal

▶ The metal from the Daleks' casings that was being used to attract the gamma radiation on the Empire State Building was named Dalekanium as previously mentioned in the 1964 story *The Dalek Invasion of Earth* [see Volume 4].

allowed the BBC team just four days use of the venue in the lead-up to their pantomime season. Following a prosthetic fitting for David Tennant for *The Family of Blood* [2007 – see Volume 56] at the actor's flat, recording at Hooverville for the conclusion of the attack took place from 4pm through the night again. On this occasion though, the crew was not as fortunate with the weather. "For five nights, it absolutely poured down," recalled Phil Collinson on the commentary. "It suited the scene and the desperation of them all," added James Strong. Amidst the mud and duckboards, the crew battled to complete the Hooverville sequences with *Doctor Who Confidential* witnessing the terrible weather conditions. The cold weather soon took its toll on David Tennant as he shouted out his required dialogue...

On the stage

Work at the theatre ran from 2pm to 1am on Wednesday 15 and focused on the dance routine which demanded three cameras as the cast mimed to a playback of a temporary version of the pre-recorded song. "We

were meant to have a glitter ball, and it didn't turn up," explained James Strong on the DVD episode commentary. Released from the shoot around 6pm, David Tennant – who by now was battling on despite problems with his voice and thus only mouthing his lines in rehearsals – attended a special photographic shoot for *Radio Times* and returned to Upper Boat for more make-up tests.

The morning of Thursday 16 November saw David missing the readthrough for *Blink* [2007 – see Volume 56] in order to rest his voice. He later joined the main unit at the theatre shortly after recording began at 2pm. The stage scenes from *Daleks in Manhattan* were completed – as covered by *Doctor Who Confidential* – and then the climactic scenes for *Evolution of the Daleks* began. Another special *Radio Times* photoshoot was conducted that evening with Eric Loren in full costume as the humanised Dalek Sec accompanied by Thay and Jast. Recording of the climax of the serial continued at the theatre from 1am to midnight on Friday 17 with Tom Lucy co-ordinating the stunt sequences.

Work on Sunday 19 November saw the crew at Headlands School in Penarth, a frequently used venue by the *Doctor Who* team since production on *The Unquiet Dead* [2005 – see Volume 48] in September 2004; on that occasion it had partially featured as Charles Dickens' dressing room, and now served the same function for Tallulah as well as providing the theatre basement. Recording ran from 11am to 10pm, with the set visited by *Torchwood* co-producer and *Doctor Who* writer Chris Chibnall and his family, *Totally Doctor Who* Companion

Left: Miranda Raison prepares to perform as showgirl Tallulah.

Academy winner Louise and presenter Kirsten O'Brien, as well as Anneke Wills who played the Doctor's companion Polly on the series from 1966 to 1967.

David Tennant was not scheduled for work at the school on Tuesday 21 as he was recording *Blink* with the Block Five crew. *Doctor Who Confidential* was present as work on staircase, corridor and dressing room scenes took place from 9.30am to 8.30pm, with Ryan Carnes finally allowed out of make-up as Laszlo for his last day, and not being recognised by any of his fellow cast members! A late addition to the script was Tallulah's comment that Heidi Chicane's broken ankle was "nothing to do with me, whatever anyone says".

"We ran out of time to shoot the descent into the manhole," recalled Phil Collinson on the *Daleks in Manhattan* commentary. Green amendments were also made to the script, omitting two short scenes of Martha chasing the Laszlo Pig along a corridor and down a staircase due to be recorded that day, and a similar sequence of the Doctor and Tallulah running along the same route due to be recorded the next day. Also dropped from the following day's work was a short scene of Tallulah deciding to follow the Doctor into the sewer from the basement.

Anniversary

Work began at Headlands School at 10am on Wednesday 22 to conclude the theatre corridor and basement scenes, with Harry Ferrier standing in for Ryan Carnes in the *Daleks in Manhattan* sequence where Martha chased Laszlo; David Tennant spoke to Miranda on her last day for his video diary. The crew then moved to Cardiff Heliport, previously used in November 2005 on *Rise of the Cybermen/The Age of Steel* [2006 – see Volume 52] and now (despite the bad weather) the venue for the erection of a six-metre tall steel and plywood-cladded structure which represented the top of the Empire State Building for the sequences of the Doctor coming round after the lightning strike, with stuntman Will Willoughby standing in for Tennant under the supervision of Tom Lucy.

Thursday 23 November – *Doctor Who*'s 43rd anniversary – saw David Tennant attending the readthrough of *Human Nature/The Family of Blood* [2007

– see Volume 56] before travelling to the heliport to record his solo mast scenes in torrential rain from 4pm to 3am, along with the scenes of the workers placing the Dalekanium in *Daleks in Manhattan* and close-ups of the hovering Daleks over Hooverville. A *TV Times* photographer was present along with the *Doctor Who Confidential* camera team and Willoughby again stood in for Tennant.

Following a shot of a Hooverville sentry recorded with Block Six on Tuesday 5 December, a series of pick-up shots were performed at Upper Boat on Friday 8 December, including explosions in the theatre, close-ups of Dalek eye stalks, the Human Dalek Sec's hands, the newspaper found by Martha and the Hybrids loading

their guns. When he was not needed for work on *Human Nature* with the main unit, David Tennant performed inserts of some specific actions on the lab set for *Evolution of the Daleks*.

CGI work at The Mill included the construction of a period New York skyline, with the team using old photos to ascertain which structures – such as the Chrysler Building – were extant in 1930; lights taken from Dave Houghton's night-time photographs were then overlayed on this for night scenes. Hovering Daleks and their firepower, further tents at Hooverville, the billboard of the Laurenzi Theatre, the harbour and the scaffolding around the Empire State Building were also added to the finished episode. ▪

PRODUCTION

Fri 13 Oct 06 Empire State Building, 350 Fifth Avenue, New York (Empire State Building)

Sat 14 Oct 06 Statue of Liberty, Liberty Island, New York (Statue of Liberty); 230 Fifth Avenue, New York (Ext Empire State Building)

Sun 15 Oct 06 Majestic Theatre, 247 West 44th Street, New York (Theatre); Central Park, Manhattan, New York (Central Park)

Mon 23 Oct 06 Upper Boat Studios, Trefforest (Empire State Building: Office)

Tue 24 Oct 06 Upper Boat Studios (Empire State Building: Office)

Wed 25 Oct 06 Upper Boat Studios (Empire State Building: Office; TARDIS)

Thu 26 Oct 06 Upper Boat Studios (Empire State Building: Lift/Office/Lift #2; Sewer Tunnel #4; Sewer Tunnel 5)

Fri 27 Oct 06 Upper Boat Studios (Sewer Tunnel #5; Sewer Tunnel #1; Sewer Tunnel #2)

Sat 28 Oct 06 Upper Boat Studios

(Sewer Tunnel #2; Sewer Tunnel #3; Sewer Tunnel #5; Sewer Tunnel #1; Sewer Tunnel #4)

Mon 30 Oct 06 Upper Boat Studios (Sewer Tunnel #3; Sewer Tunnel #5; Sewer Tunnel #4; Empire State Building – Mast/Office; Theatre; Sewer Tunnel #1)

Tue 31 Oct – Tue 7 Nov 06 Old NEG glass site, Trident Park, Glass Avenue, Cardiff Bay (Transgenic Lab)

Wed 8 Nov 06 Upper Boat Studios (Sewer Tunnel #6)

Thu 9 Nov 06 Penarth Leisure Centre, Penarth (Base of Statue of Liberty); Bute Park, Cardiff (Central Park; Solomon's Tent)

Fri 10 Nov 06 Bute Park (Central Park Hooverville)

Sat 11 Nov 06 Bute Park (Central Park – Hooverville; Woodland; Solomon's Tent)

Mon 13 – Tue 14 Nov 06 Bute Park (Central Park – Hooverville)

Wed 15 Nov 06 Park & Dare Theatre, Station Road, Treorchy (Theatre – gods/Stage)

Thu 16 Nov 06 Park & Dare Theatre (Theatre – Wings/Stage/Stalls)

Fri 17 Nov 06 Park & Dare Theatre (Theatre – Stalls/Stage)

Mon 20 Nov 06 Headlands School, St Augustine's Room. Penarth (Theatre – Basement/Tallulah's Dressing Room)

Tue 21 Nov 06 Headlands School (Theatre – Corridor #1/Staircase/Tallulah's Dressing Room/Corridor #2)

Wed 22 Nov 06 Headlands School (Theatre – Corridor #1/Basement/Corridor #2); Cardiff Heliport, Foreshore Road, Cardiff (Empire State Building – Mast)

Thu 23 Nov 06 Cardiff Heliport (Empire State Building – Top of Mast; Mast; Central Park – Hooverville)

Tue 5 Dec 06 Treberfydd House, Llangasty, Brecon (Hooverville)

Fri 8 Dec 06 Upper Boat Studios (Theatre – Stalls; Empire State Building – Office; Transgenic Lab; Base of Statue of Liberty; Sewer Tunnel #5 [inserts])

Post-production

Below:
A revolt against Sec and his modern ways is brewing.

Various trims had to be made to bring *Daleks in Manhattan* down to length, and even then the episode was one of the longest of the series. After the titles, the opening scene in the TARDIS was dropped because it felt as if the episode had two beginnings. This saw the Doctor allow Martha to take "just one more trip" before being returned home and was later included on the DVD set as a deleted scene.

The producer and director captions were superimposed on the scene of the Doctor and Martha having arrived at the foot of the Statue of Liberty. When Martha excitedly spoke of being in 1930s New York, she originally said to the Doctor,

"C'mon then, you! We need to get that ferry! Shopping, iceskating in Central Park – Broadway – where do you wanna go first?" When Solomon broke up the fight, the second man said, "I'm starving, Solomon – I got a wife and family in Queens, they rely on me to bring them somethin'..." After Solomon welcomed the Doctor and Martha to Hooverville, the Doctor explained that the pair were just visiting and had not brought food or money (later included on the DVD). Later when Martha volunteered to join the sewer gang, Mr Diagoras commented, "A lady volunteer – happy to get her hands dirty while you men sit around."

The final experiment

Having left Diagoras to move off down the tunnel, there was a short sequence with the Doctor's party removed. "I've heard stuff about New York sewers – like, they're full of alligators that people used to flush down the toilet – that's not true is it? What would they eat?" asked a nervous Martha. "They could live off the rats, plenty of them," replied the Doctor. "Okay..." said Martha as she shone her torch upwards to a shaft of daylight... and had water drip in her face to the amusement of Solomon who explained, "It's just rain off the streets. All the drains in Manhattan lead down here." At a T-junction, the Doctor then took the lead, as in the next sequence.

While Solomon watched the Doctor assembling his equipment in the theatre basement, he observed, "When I saw those pig things down there, I thought I'd walked into another world. You took it in your stride." "They've walked into your world, Solomon," replied the Doctor, "They shouldn't be here, in New York, in 1930. But if I can do one thing... then I can walk them right back out again."

Above:
March of the Human Daleks!

"Russell actually decided in the end that we didn't need them," commented James Strong on the DVD episode commentary when discussing these deleted exchanges, "and he's right; you don't need them. But at the time you think that [it should be included] because the actors did a great job."

Martha comforting Frank was also trimmed slightly, removing her saying, "Come on, Frank. Don't be scared. You're with me now." In the sewers, when Tallulah learned that the Doctor was a doctor she commented that her mom had told her to marry a doctor or a lawyer (this sequence appeared on the DVD). When he saw Martha with the party of prisoners, the Doctor exclaimed, "There she is. And Frank, he's still alive." Overhearing the Daleks, he puzzled, "Selection? What does that mean, selection for what?"

After Laszlo explained to the Doctor about the Final Experiment there was a short scene of the Black Dalek shuddering in the lab while saying, "I am... changing. I am... new. I am Dalek, reborn!" When Martha asked of the Final Experiment, "What does that mean?" in the sewer, the Dalek snapped, "Silence!" at her.

Right:
The Daleks prepare to exterminate their former leader, Sec.

Because it was the first part of a two-part story, *Daleks in Manhattan* had the trailer for *Evolution of the Daleks* placed after its closing credits, giving the continuity announcer a chance to warn that scenes from the next instalment were about to be shown.

A future without killing

Evolution of the Daleks opened with a pre-credit montage sequence leading up to the cliffhanger reprise, with the producer and director credits appearing over the opening scene of the Pig Men grabbing the prisoners. As the Doctor approached the Daleks with the radio, he originally said, "I would say, what a coincidence our meeting like this. Except I think we've gone beyond coincidence. I think you and I are bound together until the ends of time, and beyond." "Let the Doctor see the extent of his failure," said Dalek Sec, "behold the future of

the Daleks, in my shape." "Oh, you're something new, I'll give you that," replied the Doctor, in an exchange which was re-dubbed with different dialogue. When the Doctor asked Sec what his new body felt like, he replied, "So much I did not expect." "Like what?" enquired the Doctor in a tempting manner. "Do you expect me to weaken?" asked Sec. "You tell me. Go on," said the Doctor, urging the new Hybrid to, "Tell me how beautiful this feels." When speaking of 'humanity', Sec remarked, "Look at the human race, Doctor. Ravagers of their own planet! Killers of their own kind!" When Sec spoke of the pain he felt following the sonic attack, he added, "Oh, but that's *glorious*!"

The escape of the Doctor's party from the sewers into the theatre basement was omitted, with the Doctor urging the prisoners to run home; Tallulah complained about the smell while Frank realised that the Daleks would be attacking Hooverville to get replacements

'AS HE APPROACHED THE DALEKS, THE DOCTOR ORIGINALLY SAID, "I THINK YOU AND I ARE BOUND TOGETHER UNTIL THE END OF TIME."'

for their experiment and that they needed to warn Solomon (this scene was included on the DVD).

There was another scene showing the Doctor, Martha, Frank and Tallulah approaching Hooverville through the woodland, which was shot but had to be omitted from the broadcast episode because it had been recorded at the end of the day and didn't have enough coverage to be deemed transmittable. In it, Tallulah again complained about her situation, and when the others ignored her she became upset about Laszlo's fate as a pig. Solomon then approached and was overjoyed to see Frank, but the Doctor said that they had bad news for him; this scene was also included on the DVD.

Solomon's speech to the Daleks originally began, "Daleks. From what the Doctor says, you're without a home. Without friends. Without a future. Just like the men and women you see here." When the Doctor realised that Sec wanted

to change what made the Daleks behave as Daleks, Sec replied, "And you, Doctor – you must change. Put your prejudice aside. And imagine a future where the Daleks are no longer an enemy." "A future without killing," speculated the Doctor. "No, we would kill, but only as other species kill," said Sec. "We would be equals, co-existing with the rest of the universe."

In the lift, when Martha said that she, Frank and Tallulah were posing as two engineers and an architect, Tallulah said, "Oh, let me be the architect, honey. This cleavage takes work!" As the gene solution was pumped into the Hybrids, Sec announced, "The very first Daleks were born out of genetic experimentation. Now, the great work continues." Realising that Dalekanium had been added to the mast, Martha said, "Bet you a million dollars." When Laszlo grabbed the Doctor, he originally said, "I have him, my masters, the Doctor is secure." When the Daleks turned on Sec, the Human Dalek asked,

Below:
A night at the theatre, full of dramatic moments and tragedy.

"Then what happens to me, now? Are you going to kill me?" "You still contain Dalek DNA," said the second Dalek, "You can be used... We will strip your flesh. Reclaim the Dalek. Use you for breeding." When Laszlo was reunited with Tallulah, he said, "No stopping me, sweetheart. Not if it means I get to see you..."

Teeth to declare

At the theatre, when the Doctor spoke of what the Daleks had done to Sec, the Human Dalek Hybrid told the aliens to listen to the Doctor who spoke of the millions of Dalek victims who had been shown no mercy; this was included on the boxed DVD release. In the lab when Laszlo started to lose consciousness, he told the crying Tallulah, "Nothing you can do, 'Cept say goodbye. That life we had planned, sweetheart... Ain't never gonna happen." Later, in Central Park, Tallulah told Laszlo, "Hey! I can earn us some money, you ain't gonna starve, we'll be all right..." "Going back to the stage, Tallulah?" asked the Doctor. "What else?" said Tallulah, "I sing, I dance, I make people laugh, and I'm gonna keep right on doing it. Reckon this city needs it." "It does," agreed the Doctor, "Oh, this city needs you, Tallulah." Turning to Laszlo, the singer hugged him and continued, "Then we can save up, maybe get a little place some day, somewhere quiet. Cos you ain't getting rid of me, Laszlo. Not ever!"

At the start of *Daleks in Manhattan*, the music heard at the theatre was *Happy Days Are Here Again* by Milton Ager and Jack Yellen, recorded in November 1929 by Leo Reisman and his orchestra and featured in the 1930 musical *Chasing Rainbows*; this was also heard at the theatre, and then in *Evolution of the Daleks* as the music on

Left:
The Doctor checks to see if the battery is dead.

the radio. The arrival of the TARDIS in New York was backed by *Rhapsody in Blue*, George Gershwin's famous 1924 fusion of classical music with jazz. For the Doctor and Martha walking through Central Park, Irving Berlin's 1929 song *Puttin' on the Ritz* – made famous in the 1930 film of the same name – was used. Harmonica music was also played for the scene at Solomon's tent.

Automated Dialogue Replacement (ADR) recording took place on Thursday 22 February, mainly for Nicholas Briggs to re-record sections of Dalek dialogue. For post-production, Ryan Carnes had to dub most of his dialogue as Laszlo with James Strong flying out to Los Angeles to record this material.

"I had to go through US customs with the [Pig Man] teeth," Strong explained, recalling the strange reaction he received from immigration officials on his arrival. This session took place on Tuesday 13 March in a vast sound stage in Los Angeles.

James Strong recorded two online commentaries for his episodes, first for *Daleks in Manhattan* with producer Phil Collinson, then joined by editor Mike Jones for *Evolution of the Daleks*.

Publicity

▶ On Wednesday 1 November, *The Sun* ran a piece under the headline *Stunner's date with Timelord* revealing that Miranda Raison was to play 'a sexy showgirl… in an episode set in 1930s New York,' with 'an insider' commenting, "We always like to add a touch of glamour and Miranda's got it in spades." Ryan Carnes was also mentioned as appearing in the new series.

▶ The location work at Penarth Leisure Centre was covered by Molly Watson of the local paper *Western Mail* which ran the story *Doctor Who lands back in Cardiff* on Thursday 2 November.

▶ On Sunday 12 November, Rachel Richardson's piece *Dalek return* in the tabloid *News of the World* threatened to spoil the production team's careful secrecy about the Daleks up to this point.

▶ The *South Wales Echo* ran a story on Monday 13 November about eight-year-old Joshua McConkey who was off school ill, but had been taken to see the recording at Penarth Leisure Centre by his mum and got to meet the series' stars. "I like the Doctor and he was really nice and asked me my name and signed my magazines," said Joshua. "I saw some lights in the distance and it turned out to be the TARDIS!" said Gareth, an amazed inhabitant of Penarth who was a fan of the series.

▶ The presence of the Daleks in the new series of *Doctor Who* was revealed with the teaser sequence at the end of *The Runaway Bride* on Christmas Day 2006, after which *Doctor Who Magazine* released details about the two-parter and the episode title *Daleks in Manhattan*. The title of the second part, *Evolution of the Daleks,* was held back for *Radio Times* to announce in March 2007.

▶ After some discussion, on 28 March senior brand executive Edward Russell announced to licensed magazines and merchandisers that 'the Human Dalek creature for *Daleks in Manhattan/ Evolution of the Daleks* is finally known as 'Dalek Sec Hybrid' and should only be referred to by this name from now on', thus avoiding any potential racial connotations that might have been drawn from the 'Black Human Dalek' designation as used in the script.

"We love a *Radio Times* cover – how could we not?" Russell T Davies told Nick Griffiths of the striking image of Mr Diagoras as a "Half-Dalek, Half-Human, Total Monster?" on the cover of the listings magazine, despite the fact that the creature's revelation formed the climax of the unbroadcast episode. "You want to give away a certain amount to draw people in… What we try to protect are the endings of the plots – that's the important thing," Davies elaborated. Gill Hudson admitted she was "a fully paid-up member of the I Love *Doctor Who* Club" in her editorial, while the main *Doctor Who Watch* feature, *The Thinking Man's Dalek*, spanned four pages with comments from Russell T Davies on the story and Ryan Carnes and Eric Loren on their respective make-ups. Selected 'Drama of the Week',

the billing for *Daleks in Manhattan* was accompanied by a picture of the Doctor examining the genetic blob, while Mark Braxton enthused over the show's different plot elements ('the longer adventures allow the story to breathe and tensions to escalate') in *Today's Choices* along with shots of the Doctor and Martha on the Manhattan skyline and Tallulah performing on stage. The magazine also offered a packet of free stickers from the Second Edition of Merlin's collectables from the series, and a chance to claim a free album to put them in.

Above:
Radio Times reveals the Dalek/Human Hybrid.

Left:
The Doctor attempts to reason with Sec.

In the lead-up to transmission, on Friday 20 April the BBC website revealed that the Daleks had topped an online poll as the series' scariest villains, with Davies commenting of the new story, "Every time the Daleks return we make them bigger and better than ever before, and this time, their plan is the most audacious Dalek scheme yet... Even the Doctor finds himself out of his depth." On Friday morning, Nick Briggs featured on Radio Five Live's *Breakfast* programme promoting the new story, and also featured on BBC One's *Breakfast* the following day with James Strong to introduce extracts from that evening's broadcast. Production designer Edward Thomas and *Doctor Who Magazine* editor Clayton Hickman took part in a similar item about the Daleks on BBC Radio Wales on Friday afternoon. At a children's concert at St David's Hall in Cardiff, Nicholas Pegg operated a Dalek for a performance of the theme tune and incidental music from the series with Briggs having pre-recorded some Dalek dialogue.

▶ Cardiff-based paper the *Western Mail* ran a promotion of glossy double-sided *Doctor Who* posters for a week from the broadcast of *Daleks in Manhattan.*

▶ A special image of the Daleks hovering over Manhattan while lightning struck the Empire State Building was created by The Mill for a double spread in *Radio Times* introducing the *Enemy of the States* article in *Doctor Who Watch,* where Helen Raynor discussed the story with Nick Griffiths. Mark

Braxton selected *Evolution of the Daleks* as one of *Today's Choices* beneath a shot of the Doctor in the theatre; a box-out also promoted *Doctor Who Confidential* with a photo of a Dalek. The programme billing was then emphasised by another photo of the reborn Dalek Sec.

▶ The *Daily Record* ran an item about Ryan Carnes – *Happy to be a Ham Actor* by Rick Fulton – promoting *Evolution of the Daleks* on Thursday 26 April.

▶ "In a funny way, I see this as our first proper Dalek adventure," explained Davies in *Radio Times.* "Every other time they've been big, ratings-grabbing appearances. This time they've got a complicated plot. They're really clever this time..."

Broadcast

Left:
The Doctor ignores the rules and puts his feet on the seats.

≫ Allocated an extended 50-minute slot, *Daleks in Manhattan* comfortably trounced the opposition on ITV1, *Vernon Kay's Gameshow Marathon,* by over two million. The following weekend, *Doctor Who* again had a comfortable margin over ITV1's *Gameshow Marathon*. BBC Three screened the episodes again at 8pm on Sunday (a slot in which both shows topped the channel's weekly chart) and 9pm on Friday.

≫ The two editions of BBC Three's *Doctor Who Confidential* which covered the making of these episodes were entitled *A New York Story* and *Making Manhattan*; the full 45-minute versions originally aired at 7.25pm and 7.30pm following the BBC One screenings, while the 15-minute *Cutdown* versions were screened after the episode repeats later the same week.

ORIGINAL TRANSMISSION

EPISODE	DATE	TIME	DURATION	CHANNEL	RATING (CHART POSITION)	APPRECIATION INDEX
Daleks in Manhattan	21 April 2007	6.35pm-7.25pm	46'52"	BBC One	6.69M (18th)	86
Evolution of the Daleks	28 April 2007	6.45pm-7.30pm	46'24"	BBC One	6.97M (17th)	85

Merchandise

Daleks in Manhattan/Evolution of the Daleks was initially released on DVD by 2|entertain in June 2007 along with *The Lazarus Experiment* and *42* as *Series 3 Volume 2*. It was also included in *The Complete Third Series* DVD box set released in November 2007; a new commentary featuring Helen Raynor, Miranda Raison and costume designer Louise Page accompanied *Daleks in Manhattan,* while a similar track with David Tennant, Nicholas Briggs and visual effects supervisor Barney Curnow was available for *Evolution of the Daleks.* Various extended or deleted scenes from both episodes were also included as bonus features, along with the short versions of *Doctor Who Confidential*, the network trailer for *Daleks in Manhattan* and *David Tennant's Video Diary.*

Two tracks of music from *Daleks in Manhattan/Evolution of the Daleks* were included on Silva Screen's CD of *Doctor Who: Original Television Soundtrack: Series 3,*

released in November 2007; one of these was a new recording of *My Angel Put the Devil in Me* performed by Yamit Mamo. Two tracks of music from the story were also included in Silva Screen's limited edition *Doctor Who: The TARDIS Edition* released in November 2014.

In June 2007, Character Options released both a 5" and a 12" action figure of the Dalek Sec Hybrid. This was followed in July by a *Daleks in Manhattan* set of 5" action figures which included a coated Tenth Doctor, the Dalek Sec Hybrid, a Pig Man, and the damaged Dalek Thay.

In December 2008, Airfix UK released a *Daleks in Manhattan* model kit, which featured a scenario from the story. ▪

Cast and credits

CAST

David Tennant ....The Doctor
Freema Agyeman ....Martha Jones

with

Miranda Raison ....Tallulah
Ryan Carnes ....Laszlo
Hugh Quarshie .... Solomon
Andrew Garfield .... Frank
Eric Loren ....Mr Diagoras[1]/Dalek Sec[2]
Flik Swan ....Myrna[1]
Alexis Caley ....Lois[1]
Earl Perkins .... Man #1
Peter Brooke ....Man #2[1]
Ian Porter ....Foreman[1]/Hybrid[2]
Joe Montana .... Worker #1[1]
Stewart Alexander ....Worker #2[1]
Mel Taylor ....Dock Worker[1]
Barnaby Edwards, Nicholas Pegg,
Anthony Spargo[1], David Hankinson.....................
....Dalek Operators
Nicholas Briggs .... Dalek Voices
Paul Kasey ....Hero Pig Man*.
* Credited as Hero Pig in *Daleks in Manhattan*.

UNCREDITED

Victoria Southgate, Jodie Leigh, Aimee Hall,
Emma Baskerville, Mia Okorafor, Suzanne
Mole, Sarah Merry, Aimee Brammall ....
.... Chorus Girls
Ian Greenwood ....Juggler
Steve Apelt ....Clown
James Welsh, Richard Manning ....
....Stage Hands
Dinah Lees, Julian Hensey ....Passers-by
Jason Weeks ....Cyclist
Aimee Dewitt, Paul Lofts, Unknown ....
....Passers-by
Harrison Campbell, Gemma Vaughan, Carly
Puckett, Stacy Thomas, Jay Mathias ....
....Hoover Kids

Finoula Rochford, Anna Rudolph, Ellen
Florence, Vannesa Bailey, Eleanor
MacDonald ....Female Hoovers
Sean Saye, Claudio Laurini, David Handford,
Pete Symonds, Franco Demarco, John
Walker, Gary Devonish, Mark Gottshalk,
Eddie Martin, Julian Landau, Adam Barrat,
John Shepherd, Gareth Long, Christopher
Hancock, Justin Walters, Gary Greenslade ......
.... Male Hoovers (inc Jethro, Harry, Seamus)
David Morris, Andrew Morgan John .....Workers
Ruari Mears .... Pig Man
Giles Clayden, Pablo Raybould ....Body Guards
Dominic Kynaston, Simon Challis, Graham
O'Malley ....Workers
Ken Hosking, Karl Greenwood, Adam Sweet,
Kevin Hudson, Pete Symmonds............. Pig Men
Nick Madge, Tony Was, Paul Lofts,
Jonnie Black, Aimee Dewitt, Elsie May,
Julian Hensey, Annisia, Jason Weeks,
David Hodges, Tim Pottinger, Charlotte Ellis,
Lucy Eloise, Gabrielle Windsor, Julie Gregory,
Clare Brice, Carys Boulton, Angharad
Thomas, Catrin O'Neill, Jade Harris Cupit,
Aimee Baldwin, Adele Orchard, David
Brewer, Unknown, Andy Jackson, Jack
Grisham, Adam Lloyd, Mathew Riley,
Tom Welch, Oliver Gardner................... Audience
Levi Summers, Gary Dobbs, Simon Davey,
Ian Hilditch, Greg Bennett ....Prisoners
Harry Ferrier ....Double for Laszlo
Guy List ....Stunt Pig Man
Andy Smart ....Stunt Public
Kim McGarrity ....Stunt Female Hoover
Will Willoughby ....Stunt Double for The Doctor
Sabrina Morris, Will Downie, Andrew
Michell, Phil Stockton, John Jenner, Matt
Doman, Jon Lloyd, John Childs, Liam Taborn,
Alan Higgs, Matt Kid, Jason Gregg, Levi
James, Damien Mantoulan, David Stock,

Chris Barber, Jessie Mears, Louise Downie, Rebecca Tromans, Paul Anderson (Oscar) .... Human Daleks
John Gerrasio, Martin T Sherman, Laurel Lefkow, David Jarvis, Barbara Barnes, Kathryn Akin, Tim Beckman, Alan Marriott ... . Crowd ADR

CREDITS

Written by Helen Raynor
Produced by Phil Collinson
Directed by James Strong
Daleks created by Terry Nation
1st Assistant Director: Peter Bennett [uncredited: Dan Mumford]
2nd Assistant Director: Steffan Morris [uncredited Lyndsey Muir[2]]
3rd Assistant Director: Sarah Davies [uncredited: Paul Bennett[2], Glen Coxon[2]]
Location Manager: Gareth Skelding
Unit Manager: Huw Jones [uncredited: Rhys Griffiths]
Production Co-ordinator: Jess van Niekerk
Production Secretary: Kevin Myers
Production Assistant: Debi Griffiths
Production Runner: Siân Eve Goldsmith [5; uncredited on 4] [uncredited: Graham Huxtable]
Floor Runners: Heddi Joy Taylor[2], Lowri Denman, Barry Phillips[1]
Drivers: Wayne Humphreys, Malcolm Kearney
Contracts Assistant: Kath Blackman[1], Bethan Britton[2]
Continuity: Non Eleri Hughes [uncredited: Pam Humphries]
Script Editor: Lindsey Alford
Camera Operator: Roger Pearce [uncredited: John Sorapure]
Focus Puller: Steve Rees
Grip: John Robinson [uncredited: Ron Nicholls, Dai Hopkins]
Boom Operators: Jon Thomas, Bryn Thomas
Gaffer: Mark Hutchings
Best Boy: Peter Chester
Electricians: Clive Johnson, Ben Griffiths, Steve Slocombe[2]

Choreographer: Ailsa Berk
Stunt Co-ordinator: Tom Lucy [uncredited: Crispin Layfield[2]]
Stunt Performers: Andy Smart[2], Guy List[2], Will Willoughby[2]
Chief Supervising Art Director: Stephen Nicholas
Art Dept Production Manager: Jonathan Marquand Allison
Art Dept Co-ordinator: Matthew North
Chief Props Master: Adrian Anscombe
Supervising Art Director: Arwel Wyn Jones
Associate Designer: James North
Set Decorator: Julian Luxton
Standby Art Director: Lee Gammon
Design Assistants: Peter McKinstry[1], Rob Dicks[1], Ian Bunting[2], Al Roberts[2]
Cyfle Trainee: Kate Meyrick[1], Katherine Lewis[2]
Storyboard Artist: Shaun Williams[2]
Standby Props: Phil Shellard, Nick Murray
Standby Carpenter: Paul Jones
Standby Painter: Ellen Woods
Standby Rigger: Bryan Griffiths [uncredited: Neal Ruck]
Property Master: Phil Lyons
Props Buyer: Ben Morris
Props Chargehand: Gareth Jeanne[2]
Props Storeman: Martin Griffiths[2]
Forward Dresser: Amy Chandler[2]
Practical Electrician: Albert James[2]
Senior Props Maker: Barry Jones[1]
Props Makers: Penny Howarth[1], Mark Cordory[1], Nick Robatto[1]
Construction Manager: Matthew Hywel-Davies
Construction Chargehand: Allen Jones[1]
Graphics: BBC Wales Graphics
Assistant Costume Designer: Marnie Ormiston
Costume Supervisor: Lindsay Bonaccorsi
Costume Assistants: Sheenagh O'Marah, Kirsty Wilkinson
Make-Up Artists: Pam Mullins, Steve Smith, John Munro
Special Effects Co-ordinator: Ben Ashmore
Special Effects Supervisor: Paul Kelly
Special Effects Technicians: Danny Hargreaves[2], Henry Brook[2]

Prosthetics Designer: Neill Gorton
Prosthetics Supervisor: Rob Mayor
On Set Prosthetics Supervisor: Pete Hawkins[2]
  [uncredited: Peter Hawkins [1], Sarah Lockwood]
Prosthetics Technician: Matt O'Toole[2]
Casting Associate: Andy Brierley
VFX Editor: Ceres Doyle
Assistant Editor: Tim Hodges
Post-production Supervisors: Samantha Hall,
  Chris Blatchford
Post-production Co-ordinator: Marie Brown
On Line Editor: Matthew Clarke
Colourist: Mick Vincent
3D Artists: Adam Burnell[1], Jean Yves Audouard[1],
  Will Pryor[2], Mark Wallman[2], Serena
  Cacciato[2], Matthew McKinney[2]
2D Artists: Sara Bennett[1], Tim Barter[1], Adam
  Rowland[1], Joseph Courtis[1], Greg Spencer,
  Bryan Bartlett, Russell Horth, Melissa Butler-
  Adams[2], Arianna Logo[2], Simon C Holden[2]
Visual Effects Co-ordinators: Jenna Powell,
  Rebecca Johnson
On Set VFX Supervisor: Barney Curnow
Digital Matte Painters: Simon Wicker,
  Charlie Bennett, Alex Fort
Dubbing Mixer: Tim Ricketts
Supervising Sound Editor: Paul McFadden
Sound Editor: Doug Sinclair
Sound FX Editor: Paul Jefferies

Foley Editor: Kelly-Marie Angell
Finance Manager: Chris Rogers
With thanks to the BBC National Orchestra
  of Wales
Original Theme Music: Ron Grainer
Casting Director: Andy Pryor CDG
Production Executive: Julie Scott
Production Accountant: Endaf Emyr Williams
Sound Recordist: Ron Bailey
Costume Designer: Louise Page
Make-Up Designer: Barbara Southcott
Music: Murray Gold
Visual Effects: The Mill
Visual FX Producers: Will Cohen, Marie Jones
Visual FX Supervisor: Dave Houghton
Special Effects: Any Effects
Prosthetics: Millennium FX
Editor: Mike Jones
Production Designer: Edward Thomas
Director of Photography: Ernie Vincze BSC
Production Manager: Patrick Schweitzer
Executive Producers: Russell T Davies,
  Julie Gardner
BBC Wales in association with the Canadian
Broadcasting Corporation
© MMVII

[1] *Daleks in Manhattan* only
[2] *Evolution of the Daleks* only

Profile

MIRANDA RAISON Tallulah

Currently one of the UK's most in-demand actresses, Miranda Raison played her *Doctor Who* role of Tallulah in a break in filming for the BBC spy series *Spooks*, in which she starred as MI5 agent Jo Portman for five years.

Raison was born 18 November 1977 in Burnham Thorpe, Norfolk. Her father Nick is a jazz pianist and artist but it was her mother Caroline Raison, a newsreader and continuity announcer for East Anglia's ITV franchise Anglia TV, who really gave her the taste for working in television. "When my mum was a newsreader I loved all the attention she got from it," she said, recalling trips to Anglia aged five. "I enjoyed going into the studio and watching her being made-up, people buzzing round her with brushes."

Raison's parents divorced when she was six; she and her brother living with her mother. She attended primary school in Burnham Market and from the age of 10 attended five boarding schools including Gresham's School in Norfolk. While never actually expelled, she admits she could be a handful. It was during a spell at Felixstowe College that she became involved in drama and school productions. At 17 she successfully auditioned to enrol at the Webber Douglas Academy of Dramatic Art.

She made her TV début not long after graduating. An early role included a small part in two episodes of *The Inspector Lynley Mysteries* (2002). She also took a minor part in the 2005 movie *Match Point*, directed by Woody Allen. But it was playing Jo in *Spooks* (from 2005) that launched her career, a real action adventure role that also covered some harrowing ground for her character. Unfortunately for Raison's fans, Jo was killed off in 2010, although the actress left directly after filming her death scene to go to a night shoot in Leeds for six-part ITV drama *Married Single Other* (2010).

Of her part in *Doctor Who* she said: "It was a really fun part, being a showgirl and singing on the New York stage. I mean, I can't sing, so I won't have another opportunity to do that!" Directly after appearing as Tallulah she was asked if she would be interested in the lead role of Roxie in the London West End musical *Chicago* and had to admit to the producers that while she was okay with a decent microphone, she couldn't really sing like that: "Wellying out a tune in the West End, unfortunately I couldn't do!"

Opposite:
Miranda Raison as the ditzy showgirl, Tallulah.

Below:
Tallulah loves Laszlo, whatever he may look like.

Given her *Spooks* stint, Raison has since carved out a niche in genre action and fantasy shows including the role of the sword-wielding warrior Isolde in two episodes of *Merlin* (2011), *Dirk Gently* (2012), *Sinbad* (2012) and six episodes of the British-based *24* mini-series *Live Another Day* (2014).

She has also starred in *Lewis*, Yorkshire-based comedy *Sugartown* (2011), police comedy drama *Vexed* (2012) and took the regular role of Harriet Hammond in the third series of BBC legal drama *Silk* (2014). In a busy 2014, Raison shot 10-part TV series *Spotless* and filmed horror movie *AfterDeath* in her native Norfolk.

Miranda's connection with *Doctor Who* has continued with her work for Big Finish Productions. Following several guest roles in the company's range of *Doctor Who* audio dramas, Miranda accepted the regular part of Constance Clarke, a new travelling companion for the Sixth Doctor, played by Colin Baker. ∎

THE LAZARUS EXPERIMENT

> STORY 183

When the elderly Professor Lazarus
manipulates his own DNA to make him young
again, the Doctor fears the worst. It isn't
long before Lazarus undergoes a horrific
transformation into a monstrous creature!

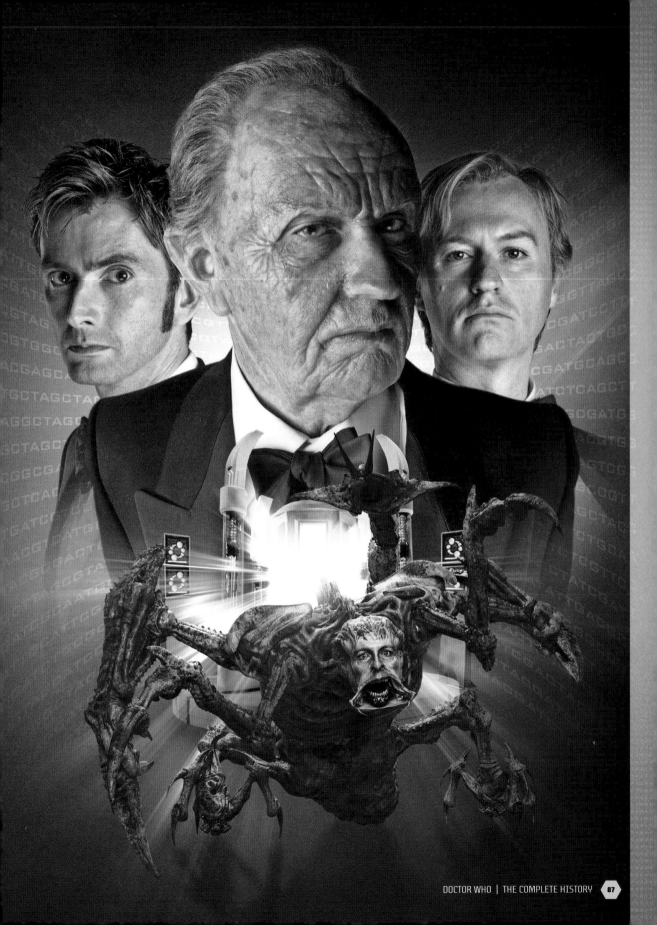

Introduction

At face value, Professor Richard Lazarus is a modern-day Dr Jekyll. And like the character from Robert Louis Stevenson's *The Strange Case of Dr Jekyll and Mr Hyde*, his experiments unleash an animalistic alter ego, which is ultimately his undoing.

It isn't, however, a mere straightforward homage. This well-trodden story of a genius scientist who develops a split personality is conflated with traditional tales about the elixir of life – an elusive cure-all that endows immortality and, in some versions, eternal youth.

Lazarus presents the Doctor with some high-minded flannel about how his extended lifespan will afford him the opportunity for further cultural and intellectual development. You would have thought such arguments would find favour with someone who is so inquisitive, and no stranger to replacing his old body for a new one himself; that the Doctor would be a hypocrite to deny others the same opportunities he enjoys. But even

setting aside the inherent dangers in the professor's experiments, the Doctor believes Lazarus is oblivious of the attendant burden and responsibilities of such extraordinary longevity. It becomes clear that the project is fuelled by narcissism. Lazarus is strongly motivated by regaining his youthful appearance and good looks. The darker side of his nature – manifested as a writhing scorpion-like colossus – is reflected in his rejuvenated human guise, as he pursues Martha's poor sister, Tish Jones, with a creepy intensity.

That vanity can be our undoing is a theme that is also explored in the Fifth Doctor's final story, *The Caves of Androzani* [1984 – see Volume 39]. In that instance, the elixir of life is a drug called Spectrox – the demand for which, results in corruption and murder. The themes of *The Lazarus Experiment* can be traced back even further, however, with both strands in evidence in stories from Tom Baker's second series. *Planet of Evil* [1975 – see Volume 24] sees a recalcitrant scientist develop a Hyde-like persona under the influence of anti-matter; *The Brain of Morbius* [1976 – see Volume 24] features an elixir of life which extends the lifespan of the Sisterhood of Karn, and is used to bring the Doctor back to life.

Stephen Greenhorn, the author of *The Lazarus Experiment*, would have been 10 years old when Tom Baker became the Doctor. Whether consciously or not, this is hardly the only time that more recent episodes have revisited ideas from this incredibly successful period of the programme, perhaps in an attempt to recapture its own youth. ■

Below:
Professor Lazarus claims that he will change what it is to be human.

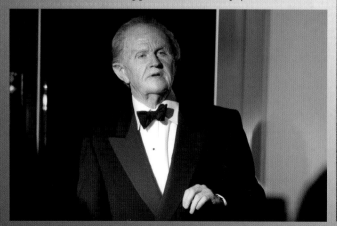

"LAZARUS IS STRONGLY MOTIVATED BY REGAINING HIS YOUTHFUL APPEARANCE AND GOOD LOOKS."

STORY

The Doctor lands the TARDIS in Martha's front room. She hears her mother leaving a message to say that her sister Tish is on television. Martha turns it on to see Tish with the elderly Professor Lazarus. He claims to have a device that will change what it means to be human. The Doctor leaves in the TARDIS – but returns a moment later, intrigued by Lazarus' device. [1]

Dressed formally, the Doctor and Martha attend a drinks reception at Lazarus Laboratories. Martha introduces the Doctor to Tish as her "plus one". Francine and Leo arrive, and Francine takes an instant dislike to the Doctor. Lazarus introduces himself and steps inside a large capsule. [2] It overloads and the Doctor is forced to unplug it. Then the capsule opens and Lazarus emerges, 40 years younger! [3]

Lazarus returns to his office with Lady Thaw and recalls sheltering in the crypt of Southwark Cathedral during the war. He recoils in disgust when she attempts to kiss him and begins to experience sharp spasms. He falls to the floor, and then a change comes over him which causes Lady Thaw to scream in terror! [4]

The Doctor and Martha examine a sample of Lazarus' DNA. The pattern keeps changing. Lazarus has activated something in his DNA that is trying to alter him. [5]

Seemingly back to normal, Lazarus returns to the reception to collect Tish. The Doctor and Martha enter Lazarus' office and discover the desiccated remains of Lady Thaw. As the Doctor and Martha leave in one lift, Lazarus and Tish emerge from the other.

The Doctor uses his sonic screwdriver to locate the energy signature of Lazarus' DNA. He's on the roof! They hurry up there to find him flirting with Tish.

Martha warns her sister to get away from him as Lazarus transforms into a hideous scorpion-like monster. [6]

The Doctor, Martha and Tish race down to the reception. A security lockdown has been triggered, sealing the exit. Martha opens it using the sonic screwdriver as the monster appears and kills one of the guests. [7] The Doctor taunts the monster to lure it after him.

It chases him through the basement as Martha helps her family and the guests to escape from the building. Then she goes back inside. Francine is approached by a Mysterious Man. [8]

The monster follows the Doctor into a laboratory, where he sets off an explosion which fails to kill it. He runs into Martha and they hide in the rejuvenation capsule. The Doctor explains that the monster is an "option that evolution rejected".

The monster activates the capsule. The Doctor rewires it to reverse the polarity, and it transforms the monster back into the apparently lifeless Lazarus. [9] Martha is reunited with her family while Lazarus is taken away in an ambulance. Seconds later, it crashes. The Doctor and Martha investigate and find two desiccated corpses within. [10]

They face the still-alive Lazarus inside the cathedral, his sanctuary. He is convinced he has now become more than just an ordinary human. The Doctor has a plan that requires Lazarus to go to the bell tower, so Martha entices him to chase her up there – but Tish comes with her. The monster traps them in the bell tower [11] as the Doctor plays the church organ, using his sonic screwdriver to "turn this thing up to 11!" [12] The noise causes the monster to fall. Lazarus is killed and turns back into an old man.

The Doctor invites Martha to resume their travels and they depart in the TARDIS. Then Francine leaves another message on Martha's machine, warning her that the Doctor will get her killed. "This information comes from Harold Saxon himself!"

Pre-production

"**M**ad scientist, present day," was Russell T Davies' brief to Stephen Greenhorn, a new writer on *Doctor Who*. "I thought he was interviewing me for the writing job, not giving me it!" Stephen later told *Radio Times*.

Having studied the arts at university, Stephen Greenhorn started writing for BBC Radio Scotland, branching out into theatre work where he made his reputation, and then contributing scripts to television series such as *The Bill* and *Where the Heart Is*. This in turn led him on to the series *Glasgow Kiss*, which Davies

had seen and enjoyed, and then creating the BBC Scotland soap opera, *River City*. When Greenhorn adapted Jean Rhys' *Wide Sargasso Sea* for the BBC, the executive producer was Julie Gardner, and in 2005 the writer enthusiastically told her how good the revived version of *Doctor Who* was and how he would love to write for it.

"My agent asked if I'd want to do something else… and I said that ideally I'd really like to do a *Doctor Who*… but that was never going to happen," recalled Greenhorn to *Doctor Who Magazine*, "I'd watched *Doctor Who* and loved it, it looked like the best thing on telly and the most fun to write for." In spring 2006,

Greenhorn's agent told him to speak to Julie Gardner, and at a meeting with Julie and script editor Simon Winstone in London on *Wide Sargasso Sea*, the possibility of him writing for *Doctor Who* was discussed. The writer then travelled to Cardiff to meet Davies where he was given a concise outline for his story. At first, Stephen had not realised that his script was required at such short notice for the 2006 series, believing it was planned for the third run of the revived *Doctor Who* in 2007; in fact, it was brought forward to replace another storyline.

Experiments gone wrong

Davies' requirement for an episode in contemporary London was to develop the storyline for Martha Jones and the rest of her family, who would return later in the series. "We did talk about where Russell wanted the arc of Martha's family to go – particularly the character of Tish," explained Stephen in *Doctor Who Magazine*. Greenhorn was provided with the scripts of *Smith and Jones* [2007 – see Volume 54] and *The Shakespeare Code* [2007 – see Volume 54] – the former giving him the background to the relationships of the Jones family – and attended a charity dinner with other writers on the series, organised by Paul Cornell, where they also talked through ideas.

Davies and Greenhorn discussed comic book and movie superheroes and villains, thinking in terms of scientist characters and the fates which befell them when their experiments went wrong. Characters from Marvel comics such as the Green Goblin (the brilliant Norman Osborn, whose strength and intelligence enhancement serum drove him insane and made him the arch-enemy of Spider-Man, created

for *Amazing Spider-Man* in 1964) and the Hulk (physicist Dr Bruce Banner's brutish alter-ego after being caught in the blast of his own gamma bomb, débuting in *Incredible Hulk* in 1962) were discussed, although the key reference point became Doctor Octopus – an enemy introduced in *Amazing Spider-Man* in July 1963 – whose mechanical arms were fused to him following a lab accident. One early notion was that the scientist would develop an impervious super-skin for military use, but Davies feared this might be too close to the next *Spider-Man* movie.

Some of the ideas discussed about experiments going wrong were dropped as they were too similar to narratives being used in *Torchwood*. "I was thinking about films like *The Fly*, examples from literature like Jekyll and Hyde, and the Faust legend," Greenhorn told *Doctor Who Magazine* as the experimentation notion was considered. *The Fly* was a short science-fiction story by George Langelaan published in *Playboy* in June 1957 which told of André Delambre, a scientist whose matter transference experiments went wrong when his body was mixed with that of a fly, turning him

Below: Martha introduces her sister Tish to the Doctor.

Above:
There's a
monster on the
loose in the
cathedral.

into a monster; this had been popularised as a 1958 horror film, in turn remade in 1986. *The Strange Case of Dr Jekyll and Mr Hyde* is an 1886 novella by Robert Louis Stevenson in which Dr Henry Jekyll developed a potion to divide his two different characteristics, the evil side of his persona becoming Edward Hyde.

Eventually, the experiment was refined into the notion of a rejuvenating machine which gave a strong motivation for Lazarus; "He's a human who only wants to be young," explained Davies on *Doctor Who Confidential*. This also allowed Greenhorn to dramatically explore the notion of longevity from the different standpoints of Lazarus and the Doctor. Originally called Professor Anger, Lazarus was named after the biblical figure that Jesus raised from the dead in the book of John; hence in the script the Doctor noted that he should have expected the professor to come back to life. Two-thirds of the way through the writing process, Russell asked Stephen to

Connections: Sound effect
▶ Playing the organ, the Doctor's comment, "Turn this thing up to 11!" came from the custom amplifier setting in the 1984 spoof rockumentary *This Is Spinal Tap*.

make Lazarus sponsor the mysterious Harold Saxon, setting up the project as a potential plot element featuring the Master for the end of the series.

The final showdown

In its very early stages, Stephen Greenhorn developed a storyline set in the London landmark of the Thames Flood Barrier, but this had to be dropped because the setting had already been earmarked for the next Christmas special. Instead, the script originally led up to a climax in St Paul's Cathedral, with Lazarus' office overlooking the Baroque edifice designed by Sir Christopher Wren and completed in 1708. But there were to be problems with the venue. Speaking to *Doctor Who Magazine*, Russell T Davies explained: "They were very kind, and even regretful, but had genuine worries about the death of someone falling from the Whispering Gallery."

"[They] pulled out on us at the last minute and we had to re-jig everything, and there were elements in the plot to do with this location, so they all got ripped out at the last minute," explained Greenhorn in *Doctor Who Magazine*. The main casualties were references to the Doctor having known Sir Christopher Wren, along with elements of the cathedral's survival through the Second Great Fire of London during the Blitz in December 1940. St Martin-in-the-Fields and the Albert Hall were approached as alternative venues and both were receptive, but the production team felt that they lacked the sense of 'sanctuary'.

The Lazarus Experiment was to be made as part of the third recording block along with *Gridlock* [2007 – see page 6] and directed by Richard Clark. At the tone meeting on Wednesday 16 August, Russell

"WHILE WE'VE ALWAYS WANTED TO CAST MARK AS SOMETHING, WE NEVER WANTED TO WASTE HIM BY GIVING HIM A CAMEO FOR THREE SCENES."

T Davies told the team that, "Our starting point here is Marvel Comics." It was considered at first that two similar actors could play the young and aged versions of Lazarus, unless an actor used to prosthetic work was cast. This latter option was soon felt to be the best solution, recalling Millennium FX's successful work in ageing Paul Whitehouse for the 2005 comedy series *Help*. As for the Lazarus creature, "I thought it was time to ask The Mill for a really lively, big, cumbersome but lithe creature that could move like lightning, strike people down and have a huge presence on the set," said Davies on *Doctor Who Confidential*.

The script reached its seventh draft on Friday 25 August and was issued as a shooting script on Wednesday 6 September. A late addition to the script was the opening TARDIS scene, requested by Russell T Davies, in which the Doctor originally told Martha that she had reached her "ultimate destination"; Martha did not refer to visiting New New York from *Gridlock*, but only meeting Shakespeare in *The Shakespeare Code* and going to New York in *Daleks in Manhattan/Evolution of the Daleks* [2007 –

Below:
Tish isn't into the older gentleman.

see page 38]. The script specified Martha watching Tish on BBC News 24 (as seen in episodes like *Aliens of London* [2005 – see Volume 49]). Professor Richard Lazarus was introduced as 'a wizened old man in his 70s' while Lady Sylvia Thaw was 'a flinty old lady in her seventies'. It was Lady Thaw who referred to Mr Saxon, the character planned for the final episodes of the run. Tish's full first name was defined as Patricia, changed in later dubbing to Letitia.

Mysterious Man

Seeing the Doctor in a tuxedo, Martha compared him to the famous fictional secret agent James Bond, created by Ian Fleming in 1953. The Genetic Manipulation Device was 'a walk-in capsule no bigger than a phone box. Four large arms curve up from the floor to meet at a point above the capsule – like two intersecting arches describing quarter segments of a dome.' When Tish was introduced to the Doctor, she originally said, "You're actually qualified then? That's good. It's about time [Martha] stopped wasting her time with students." When emphasising her role to her sister, Tish explained that she was, "Senior PR assistant, actually. Twenty-nine grand a year, six weeks holiday and a clothing allowance." "That's impressive," said a surprised Doctor, "for someone your age." "Don't sound so shocked," said an indignant Tish, "They recognised my potential, that's all." After Tish left the pair, when Martha asked what they should do next, the Doctor replied, "Mingle. Mingle and nibble," grabbing a vol-au-vent and commenting, "French, you know. Means 'flight of the wind'." "If you eat any more of those prawn ones, you might be demonstrating that, rather than translating it," observed Martha.

Above: Francine is worried that Martha is not safe with the Doctor.

When Francine and Leo arrived, Francine asked her daughter, "Is everything alright?... You seem different. Has something happened? Are you sure you're okay?" "Positive," said Martha, evasively. Lazarus' speech referred to Ernest Rutherford, the New Zealand-born father of nuclear physics who split the atom at the start of the twentieth century, and Neil Armstrong's Apollo 11 moon landing in July 1969. Later, when Lady Thaw said she aimed to exploit the process commercially, Lazarus explained, "We want everyone to benefit from this." "If they can afford it," added Lady Thaw. "But that's insane!" exclaimed Martha. "If you extend life expectancy it has huge effects on population and resources." Originally, Lazarus told Lady Thaw that he grew up in a tiny flat over a bookshop, although this was later changed to a butcher's shop in reference to Hilary Briss, a character that Mark Gatiss, cast as Lazarus, had played in his comedy series *The League of Gentlemen*. Lazarus also spoke of Southwark Cathedral on the south bank of the River Thames, the oldest Gothic church in the city, built around the thirteenth century.

The Mysterious Man who spoke to Francine about the Doctor was not in the original script, only being added after the

readthrough at the request of Russell T Davies, and the dialogue with the Jones family at the reception was reworked. Originally Francine asked, "Who is this Doctor anyway?" "I don't know," replied Tish, "someone from the hospital, I presume." "Have you heard about him before?" asked Francine, "Has she ever mentioned him?... She seems to know him very well. So why's she been keeping him a secret?" "Maybe the girl just wants her privacy," suggested Leo. Later on, Leo asked Martha if she was trying to avoid Tish, who was looking for her, and then told Martha and the Doctor that Tish had gone upstairs with Lazarus.

Originally, Tish asked Martha if she was drunk during the roof top scene, and then remarked, "You can't stand it when I'm happy can you?" Of the age gap between her and Lazarus, Tish made a reference to Welsh actress Catherine Zeta-Jones, who married actor Michael Douglas, 25 years her senior, in 2000. When Lazarus changed into the creature, Martha explained,

Connections: Technobabble

❯ Emerging from the GMD, the Doctor explained that he was a bit out of practice when it came to "reversing the polarity", a bit of technobabble which had been associated with the Third Doctor as played by Jon Pertwee in serials like *Terror of the Autons* [1971 - see Volume 16] and *The Sea Devils* [1972 - see Volume 18].

Above:
Francine is given some disturbing news by the Mysterious Man.

"That's your boss." "In that case, I quit!" said Tish. The female guest who argued with the Doctor originally simply told him, "The only danger here is you causing panic." Originally the Doctor drew the Lazarus creature away from a waitress whom the colossus had trapped under a table, rather than the concussed Leo, and Martha helped the girl escape, passing her into the care of Tish. When Martha said she was going back for the Doctor and her mother claimed that her new friend had changed her, Martha agreed, "Yeah. It's the Doctor. He's the reason. That's why I'm not leaving him… Look after Leo. I'll come find you. I promise." Again, the Jones family dialogue outside LazLabs was different, lacking the presence of the Mysterious Man, but with Francine increasingly curious about the Doctor.

Connections: Roll over…

❯ The Doctor remarks that he hung around with eighteenth-century German composer and pianist Ludwig van Beethoven (1770 - 1827), who began to lose his hearing in his late 20s.

Francine did not originally slap the Doctor, but said, "I don't know whether I should be thanking you for saving my daughter's life or slapping you for putting it at risk." In the revised script, after being slapped the Doctor made a reference to Rose's mum, Jackie Tyler, slapping him in *Aliens of London*.

At the end of the script, Francine's message was originally, "I'm worried about you. I don't like what's been happening with that Doctor. I don't think you're safe. Do you hear me?… Martha?" The final reference to Mr Saxon – now named Harold Saxon – was another late addition, inserted by Davies into the Additional Dialogue Recording script to tie in with the new scenes featuring the Mysterious Man and the series' overall arc.

The events of the episode began with the TARDIS landing on Day 7 – the morning after Martha had accompanied the Doctor in the TARDIS at the end of Episode 1 – and continued throughout Night 7. The description of the Lazarus creature was vague in the original shooting script, noting that it had a stinging tail which it used to reduce its victims to husks. The amalgam creature was worked out in conjunction with The Mill, and at one point it was suggested that the monster would keep flashing into different forms such as bat, bird or lizard. Russell T Davies then drew a sketch of how he envisaged the creature for Dave Houghton of The Mill to develop.

Perfect casting

Although all the cast for *Gridlock* was in place for the Block Three readthrough on the evening of Monday 11 September, *The Lazarus Experiment* had yet to be fully cast, meaning that David Tennant and Freema Agyeman found themselves performing Greenhorn's script with the production team.

The guest cast was finalised in the coming weeks, with successful writer-performer Mark Gatiss playing Richard Lazarus. A great devotee of *Doctor Who*, Gatiss was best known for his work with The League of Gentlemen comedy group, but had written *Doctor Who* novels and audio dramas as well as the scripts for the TV episodes *The Unquiet Dead* [2005 – see Volume 48] and *The Idiot's Lantern* [2006 – Volume 52]. He had also served as the narrator for the second series of *Doctor Who Confidential*. "While we've always wanted to cast him as something, we never wanted to waste him by giving him a cameo as an eccentric Oxford don for three scenes before he's murdered," said Russell T Davies in *Doctor Who Magazine*. The role of Lazarus would require an actor used to wearing prosthetics, for which Gatiss qualified after playing many bizarre characters as part of the League. "It's an absolute dream part because it's three monsters in one," said Gatiss on *Doctor Who Confidential*, "I'd always hoped if I got to be in the show it would be something juicy like this." This also meant that Mark would be working with his old friend David Tennant with whom he had previously worked on audio drama projects for Big Finish and the BBC Four live remake of *The Quatermass Experiment* in 2005. Davies saw Gatiss as perfect casting, telling *Doctor Who Confidential* that, "He just understands *Doctor Who* so well. Pitching a villain just right is so important." Although he often attended *Doctor Who* readthroughs for other episodes, Mark was busy on another project in Bristol and so was unable to attend the readthrough of the episode in which he was starring.

Gatiss was announced to the press on Thursday 28 September along with Thelma Barlow, best-known for playing Mavis Riley in *Coronation Street* from 1971 to 1997. "I haven't played anything quite like her before," the actress told *Doctor Who Magazine*, "but I've always wanted to play Lady Macbeth, and Lady Thaw has that same sort of ruthlessness." ■

Above:
Old friends Mark Gatiss and David Tennant had the pleasure of working together again.

Production

> "IT'S STRANGE FINALLY TO BE IN IT, AFTER ALL THESE YEARS OF WANTING TO BE IN IT."

Monday 2 October, the final day allocated to *Gridlock*, saw Richard Clark's main unit working at Upper Boat while another unit recorded the scenes with the regular cast – David Tennant, Freema Agyeman and all the members of the Jones family – on location. Next evening, Mark Gatiss joined David, Freema and Gugu Mbatha-Raw to travel to Wells in Somerset for two nights' recording for the climax of the episode. Standing in for Southwark

Cathedral, Wells Cathedral dates from the late twelfth and early thirteenth centuries and has often featured in period, rather than present day, productions. The crew was based at the EMI Sports and Social Club on Chamberlain Street, and recording ran through the night from 9pm to 6am; indeed nearly the entire episode was to be recorded at night. On the first night, the early sequences of the Doctor's party confronting Lazarus were recorded with scenes in the first tower gallery and stairway. Although the Doctor was dressed in his 'unlucky' DJ, this was

in fact a nicer suit than the nylon one that David Tennant had worn in the previous series. "It's strange finally to be in it, after all these years of wanting to be in it," Mark Gatiss told *Doctor Who Confidential* of his first appearance in *Doctor Who...* for which he was wearing his Dr Chinnery wig from *The League of Gentlemen*. He also relished working with David Tennant. "I've known David for years now – he's one of my oldest friends – and I also know quite a lot of the crew, so in some ways it was just like any other shoot... business as usual," the actor told *Radio Times*. Mark spent some time chatting to David for his DVD video diary during the night.

The episode was a chance for Freema to enjoy a change of outfit. "It was so nice to get to wear something different," Freema commented on *Totally Doctor Who*, "I love Martha's classic look, but it was just so lovely to put on that evening dress."

Work at Wells concluded with a session from 7pm to 3am on Wednesday 4 October on the organ scenes and the demise of Lazarus. *Doctor Who Confidential* was present, as was David Bednall, an organist who advised on David

Above:
It's been an evening of surprises for the Doctor and the Joneses.

Tennant's playing of the instrument and performed all the close-ups of the Doctor's hands. For Lazarus' death, Gatiss lay naked on the cathedral's stone slabs, kept warm between takes with a large onesie.

The next major venue for the episode was the Senedd, the Welsh National Assembly building in Cardiff, where Lazarus would hold his reception. "It's an iconic building in Cardiff and by far the most hi-tech and modern building there is," explained Richard Clark in *Doctor Who Confidential*. The venue was designed by Richard Rogers and was formally opened by the Queen on Wednesday 1 March 2006. With the crew

based at the WDA Compound at Cardiff Docks, recording took place over several nights from 7pm to 6am, mainly in the transparent public level of the Neuadd. "They were so helpful to us," said Russell T Davies of the Senedd's owners on *Doctor Who Confidential*. The first night's work on Thursday 5 October saw Mark Gatiss performing the reception room scenes as the rejuvenated Lazarus, with Reggie Yates and Adjoa Andoh rejoining the cast. The following night, Friday 6, Gatiss was not needed on location as the chaos of the Lazarus creature in the reception area was recorded. For this action scene, the cast was shown sketches and a rough animation of the monster so they could plan how to react, while a green ball on the end of a stick was used to give the guests an eye line on the as-yet non-existent horror; a polecam

Connections: Dressing up

▶ Wearing formal black tie, the Doctor says that something bad always happened when he is in such attire. This is a reference to the Cyberman attack in *Rise of the Cybermen* [2006 – see Volume 52].

was also used for high-angle shots of the mutant's point of view. *Doctor Who Confidential* was on set to show Any Effects detonating lightweight collapsible tables, and Charles Jarman standing in for Reggie Yates when Leo was hit by a table.

Quite freaky

Over the weekend on Sunday 8 October, the charity concert of *Doctor Who: A Celebration* was announced for the following month. Work at the Senedd resumed on the night of Monday 9, this time with Mark Gatiss in full prosthetic as the elderly Lazarus for the first time. The application of this took around three hours, and a new prosthetic was needed every day. Millennium had crafted this on a cast of the actor, but had also used a bust of the late horror film actor Vincent Price for some of the wrinkly detail. This application by Neill Gorton and Sarah Lockwood, along with contact lenses from Richard Glass, was completed with a wig

and further prosthetics to age Gatiss' hands; the actor also wore cataract contact lenses and false teeth. "It feels like skin. It's warm to touch," the actor told *Doctor Who Confidential*, noting that as he would reach his 40th birthday on Tuesday 17 it was "a terrifying glimpse of the future". *Doctor Who Confidential* was present to see the cast's reaction to Mark Gatiss in full make-up; "It's really quite freaky talking to you like that," exclaimed David Tennant. Scenes recorded that night covered the Doctor and Martha arriving at the reception. Gatiss was also in full prosthetic again the next night – Tuesday 10 – for scenes of Lazarus meeting the Doctor and the demonstration of his machine, as well as the completion of Martha getting the guests to safety. This also saw the appearance of the Mysterious Man. Benjamin Cook from *Doctor Who Magazine* and writer Stephen Greenhorn were both present, while Mark

Connections: Lights out!

❯ When speaking to Lazarus, the Doctor says he was at the Blitz in London, referring to his visit in *The Empty Child/The Doctor Dances* [2005 - see Volume 50].

Below left: The bloom of youth is upon Professor Lazarus once more.

Below right: "That's an interesting perfume. What's it called?"

Gatiss christened Lazarus' female lab assistant 'Helga'.

With the supporting artist-heavy reception scenes completed, a smaller cast returned to the Senedd on Wednesday 11 October to record the Doctor and Martha entering Lazarus' capsule (a re-dressed version of the descent capsule from *The Impossible Planet* [2006 – see Volume 53]) and the scientist's apparent demise. Following this, the crew relocated to the roof of Churchill House on Churchill Way in Cardiff to record the skyline transformation of Lazarus.

Blown off his feet

The final night at the Senedd, on Thursday 12, saw work from 6.30pm to 5.30am covering the Doctor being pursued by Lazarus through a storeroom, and then the scenes with the lifts and stairwell, before further corridor scenes around the building where the Doctor met Martha during the chase. Friday 13 then saw two units working at Lloyds TSB in Cardiff; a second unit recorded sequences with Gugu outside for *Smith and Jones* during the day, and then from 6.30pm the main unit covered scenes in Lazarus' office. Gatiss began in elderly make-up – also

Opposite:
The Doctor, Tish and Martha search for Lazarus in Southwark Cathedral.

Opposite bottom:
Lady Thaw soon discovers that young men can be cruel.

Left:
Lazarus is not the man he once was.

recording his dying insert with the Doctor for the cathedral – and then becoming youthful again as dawn approached; this was again covered by David in his video diary.

Following a readthrough for Block Four at the Holland House Hotel that afternoon, recording on *The Lazarus Experiment* resumed at 5pm at the Cardiff National Museum, part of the Edwardian civil complex in Cathays Park. The *Doctor Who Confidential* camera crew got in on the act as the film crew covering the aged Lazarus' broadcast at the start of the show. Vehicles such as an ambulance, a taxi and a Bentley were needed for the scenes out on the street, with stunt co-ordinator Tom Lucy supervising Francine slapping the Doctor. In the early hours, scenes in the laboratory foyer and security station were recorded.

Work on Tuesday 17 started at 4.30pm at Upper Boat to record the shot of the Doctor being blown off his feet by the explosion behind him. Tom Lucy again supervised this stunt, checking the distance and heat himself in rehearsals and then coaching David Tennant for his performance of the stunt; the actor was protected with fire retardant gel on the back of his head and neck. *Doctor Who Confidential* again captured this iconic set piece before work continued with greenscreen inserts for the roof scenes, and then David and Freema went to a biosciences lab at Cardiff University to record the

Connections: Wise words

❯ Lazarus quotes American writer TS Eliot's 1925 modernist poem *The Hollow Men*: "Between the idea and the reality/ Between the motion and the act" with the Doctor concluding, "Falls the shadow." The Doctor later quotes Eliot again from the final stanza of the poem, "This is the way the world ends/Not with a bang but a whimper."

"I HAVEN'T PLAYED ANYTHING QUITE LIKE HER BEFORE, BUT I'VE ALWAYS WANTED TO PLAY LADY MACBETH, AND LADY THAW HAS THAT SAME SORT OF RUTHLESSNESS."

scenes in the Lab Room through to 3.30am.

Freema and Gugu recorded the greenscreen shots in the High Gallery of the cathedral at Upper Boat from 3pm on Wednesday 18 under the auspices of Tom Lucy and *Doctor Who Confidential*. Meanwhile, David Tennant worked with a second unit on inserts for *Gridlock*, being released at 6pm. After this, the unit continued with inserts for *The Lazarus Experiment* showing three 'horrified beautiful guests' at the reception (second assistant director Jennie Fava, production manager Tracie Simpson and make-up artist Steve Smith), a shot of steam in the storeroom and the shadow of Lazarus transforming. The final day of Block Three was Thursday 19 with recording from 1.30pm to 12.30am involving only David and Freema. Work began on the set of Martha's flat for both *Smith and Jones* and *The Lazarus Experiment*, followed by a close-up of the Doctor for *The Runaway Bride* [2006 – see Volume 54] and then the scenes inside the capsule for *The Lazarus Experiment*. "We weren't actually that close," explained Freema of the machine interior on *Totally Doctor Who*, "There was plenty of

Above: Lady Thaw has had the life drained out of her.

room all around us. I think [David] might have got a little electric shock at one point, which made me laugh."

Originally planned for Thursday 19 October, the TARDIS scene which opened the episode had been deferred during production and was recorded along with another sequence destined for *Blink* [2007 – see Volume 56] at Upper Boat on Tuesday 7 November, plus various inserts for *Smith and Jones* and shots of Lazarus' jacket ripping as he transformed. ■

PRODUCTION

Tue 3 Oct 06 Wells Cathedral, Cathedral Green, Wells (Cathedral; First Tower Gallery; Stairway)

Wed 4 Oct 06 Wells Cathedral (Cathedral; Cathedral - Organ; First Tower Gallery)

Thu 5-Fri 6 Oct 06 Welsh National Assembly Building, Pierhead Street, Cardiff (Reception Room)

Mon 9-Tue 10 Oct 06 Welsh National Assembly Building (Reception Room)

Wed 11 Oct 06 Welsh National Assembly Building (Reception Room); Churchill House, Churchill Way, Cardiff (Roof)

Thu 12 Oct 06 Welsh National Assembly Building (Storeroom; Storeroom Corridor; Corridor to Lazarus' Office; Stairwell; Corridor) Fri 13 Oct 06 Lloyds TSB, Tresillian Way, Cardiff (Lazarus' Office; Cathedral)

Mon 16 Oct 06 Cardiff National Museum, Museum Avenue, Cardiff (Ext

Lazarus' Laboratory; London Street; The Foyer; Security Station)

Tue 17 Oct 06 Upper Boat Studios, Trefforest (Corridor; Roof); Biomedical Science Building, Museum Avenue, Cardiff (Lab Room)

Wed 18 Oct 06 Upper Boat Studios (High Gallery; Reception; Storeroom; Lazarus' Office)

Thu 19 Oct 06 Upper Boat Studios (Living Room – Martha's Flat; Capsule)

Tue 7 Nov 06 Upper Boat Studios (TARDIS)

Post-production

Photographs of Mark Gatiss had been taken against a greenscreen during production and these were used to create a version of Lazarus' face on his monstrous alter-ego. The Mill also created the spinning effect of the GMD, the new laboratory exterior placed on the building exterior, and added in the bell and dizzying drop at the top of the tower in Southwark Cathedral.

For the episode's music score, Murray Gold came up with a new arrangement of his theme for Martha from *Smith and Jones* which would be played by the string quartet at the reception, while at the *Doctor Who: A Celebration* concert on Sunday 19 November, compère David Tennant teased the audience with details of Professor Lazarus' Genetic Manipulation Device –

"but you don't know about that one yet..."

The working title for the episode had been *The Madness of Professor Lazarus*, but in December the episode was given the title *The Lazarus Experiment*. "The title isn't a homage to [Nigel Kneale's 1953 BBC science-fiction serial] *The Quatermass Experiment*," explained Davies. "It didn't even occur to me. It's just a good title!"

The opening producer and director captions were shown over an establishing shot of the reception room. Of the trims made to bring the episode down to time, before Martha's landline rang, her mobile chimed and, noting that it was Leo, she switched if off, telling the Doctor, "My brother. He'll call back if it's important." Talking to Lazarus before the demonstration, Lady Thaw originally stated, "My concern is financial." On their

Right:
The Doctor uses the sonic to scan for the resurrected Lazarus.

way to the reception, while Martha was concerned about her dress, the Doctor was delighted to find the first draft of the United States Declaration of Independence in his pocket and reminisced about Thomas Jefferson, the third president of the USA who had been involved in the famous 1776 document; this exchange was included as a bonus on the boxed DVD release. Entering the reception, the Doctor spotted the GMD and commented, "Now that looks interesting." "Must be the device Lazarus was talking about. What do you think it does?" asked Martha. "Well, if I had to speculate, I'd say the number of possible applications is dependent on a pretty large set of variables," replied the Doctor. "You don't know," deduced Martha. "No idea," said the Doctor as the nibbles came past. Meeting Tish, Martha originally said, "Thanks for squeezing us on to the guest list." "Well, it's a special occasion isn't it?" said her sister.

Best interests

When the Doctor asked about the experiment, Tish bluffed her way, saying, "It's highly confidential. I can only discuss it with authorised personnel – *ie* not you. It's going to change the world though. Just think, you'll actually get to see history made, in person!"

Speaking to the guests, Lazarus announced, "I have developed a device which offers us a future free of disease and affliction. A future where we can control our fate and realise our limitless potential." Martha asked the Doctor if Lazarus' claim of changing the world for ever was serious, to which the Doctor replied, "I'm afraid so." Standing beside Lady Thaw, Tish

asked, "He has done this before, hasn't he?" as the experiment began. "Would you want to go through this more than once?" asked Lady Thaw. Speaking to Lady Thaw about the Blitz, Lazarus recalled, "The destruction was incredible. Huge areas were reduced to rubble. A wasteland." When the youthful Lazarus took Tish away from the party at the reception, he said, "Thank you for rescuing me." "I'm sorry," said Tish, "I should have been paying attention. I didn't realise those people were causing a problem for you." "No. No problem," said Lazarus, "But it's nice to know that someone has my best interests at heart." "Thank you," said the flattered Tish, "It's my job. I try to do my best." "I've always valued dedication," said the professor, "I look out for it in people. It's a rare thing these days." When Tish said she would always be there if he needed anything, Lazarus flirted, "That's a comforting thought. I'll remember that."

When the Doctor and Martha entered Lazarus' office, Martha spotted lipstick on one of the glasses on the desk, commenting, "He's been here. And had a woman with him." "Well," said the Doctor, "I suppose if you suddenly acquired a body like that you might want to test drive it a bit." Charged with getting the guests to safety, Martha originally yelled, "Listen to me! If you panic, more people will die. You've got to stop pushing, stay calm and keep moving. Do you hear me?" As the guests responded, she continued, "That's it. We're all going to get out of here. Just keep calm." At the crashed ambulance, Martha told Tish to go back and stay with her Mum and Leo, but Tish replied, "It was mum who sent me. I'm supposed to keep you out of trouble."

Will Cohen from The Mill and Reggie Yates recorded an episode commentary for the BBC website. ∎

Publicity

Right:
Thelma Barlow
plays a very
different role to
her *Coronation
Street*
character.

Below:
Martha ignores
the warnings of
her mother and
continues her
travels with the
Doctor.

▶ *Who's Scariest Monster Yet?* asked *Doctor Who Watch* in *Radio Times* as Nick Griffiths and Barry McIlheney spoke to Stephen Greenhorn, Russell T Davies and Mark Gatiss about Lazarus and his alter ego. More free stickers were pasted to the feature page, while Mark Braxton described the 'pretty conventional runaround' as a homage to *She* (H Rider Haggard's 1886/7 serial about a sorceress called Ayesha who renewed herself in a flame of immortality), *The Fly* and *The Quatermass Experiment* (in which the sole survivor of Britain's first spaceshot mutates into a horrific creature with a climax in Westminster Abbey) on the *Today's Choices* page, where the show was emphasised by a large colour shot of the Doctor and Martha all dressed for the reception. The listing itself was graced with a shot of Martha, while elsewhere in the issue, BBC Creative Director Alan Yentob declared that "*Doctor Who* is one of the few shows that the family will sit down and watch".

▶ Bad news for *Doctor Who* fans was formally announced on Wednesday 2 May 2007; BBC One had decided that with the scheduling of the Eurovision Song Contest on Saturday 12 May, the episode *42* would be deferred by a week. As such, the trailer for *42* at the end of *The Lazarus Experiment* was removed and replaced by a montage of scenes from the remaining episodes, originally intended as a red button bonus, with the caption, 'Coming Up...' – after which the next caption explained 'Dr Who will return in two weeks'. The trailer featured on the BBC's red button service at various points over the next fortnight.

▶ On Wednesday 2 May, Thelma Barlow appeared on *The New Paul O'Grady Show* on Channel 4 where a clip from her forthcoming episode was screened, and did some similar promotion on ITV1's *This Morning* next day.

▶ On Saturday 5 May, *The Sun* carried Nadia Mendoza's *Who's up for a fight, Doctor?* in which Mark Gatiss commented about that night's instalment and his love for the series.

"DOCTOR WHO IS ONE OF THE FEW SHOWS THAT THE FAMILY WILL SIT DOWN AND WATCH."

THE LAZARUS EXPERIMENT ▶ STORY 183

Broadcast

The Doctor and the family Jones.

▶ Broadcast, rather aptly, the day after Boots started selling its much-hyped anti-ageing cream No7 Protect & Perfect Beauty Serum, *The Lazarus Experiment* was broadcast on BBC One in the series' usual 7pm slot. Again, *Doctor Who* comfortably won its timeslot against *Vernon Kay's Gameshow Marathon* on ITV1. David Tennant watched the broadcast of the episode at the home of Mark Gatiss.

▶ As usual, the episode was repeated during the following week on BBC Three at 8pm on Sunday 6 May and 9pm on Friday 11 May. BBC Three aired the full version of *Monsters Inc.*, the *Doctor Who Confidential* which went behind the scenes of the episode, at 7.45pm after the BBC One broadcast the shorter *Cutdown* versions scheduled after the two repeats during the week.

ORIGINAL TRANSMISSION

EPISODE	DATE	TIME	CHANNEL	DURATION	RATING (CHART POSITION)	APPRECIATION INDEX
The Lazarus Experiment	Saturday 5 May 2007	7.00pm-7.45pm	BBC One	43'27"	7.19M (12th)	86

Merchandise

The Lazarus Experiment was initially released on DVD by 2|entertain in June 2007 along with *Daleks in Manhattan/ Evolution of the Daleks* and *42* as *Series 3 Volume 2*. It was also included in *The Complete Third Series* DVD box set released in November 2007; this version included a commentary from

David Tennant and Mark Gatiss recorded on Wednesday 20 June 2007 and also an extended scene along with the short version of *Doctor Who Confidential* and the network trailer plus *David Tennant's Video Diary*. The episode also retained the unbroadcast *Next Time...* teaser trailer for *42*. ■

Below:
Behind the scenes on *The Lazarus Experiment* with *Doctor Who Confidential*.

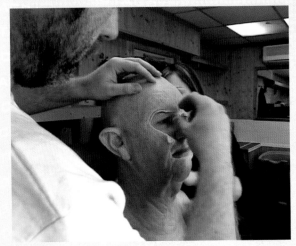

Cast and credits

CAST

David Tennant	The Doctor
Freema Agyeman	Martha Jones
with	
Gugu Mbatha-Raw	Tish Jones
Reggie Yates	Leo Jones
Adjoa Andoh	Francine Jones
Mark Gatiss	Lazarus
Thelma Barlow	Lady Thaw
Lucy O'Connell	Olive Woman[1]
Bertie Carvel	Mysterious Man.

[1] Billed as Party Guest in *Radio Times*

UNCREDITED

4 Unknown members of *Doctor Who Confidential* Film Crew

Paul Bird, John Blackwood, Hugh McInally ....Security

Malcolm Kearny, Wayne Humphreys ....Drivers

Jo Buckland, Sue Lord, Rebekah Brown .... String Quartet - Violin

Victoria Wadey ....String Quartet – Cello

Joseph Lippiatt, Adam White ....Waiters

Maria Ohrwall, Alice Mundy ....Waitresses

Greg Bennett, Richard Shaw, Roger Francis, Gavin Hesketh, Richard Price, Mark Soffe, Gemma Murcott, Mandy Garrigan ....Photographers

Greg Bowler, Mark Francis, George Nelson, Justin Claridge, Neil Duffin, Damian Edwards, Gareth Edwards, Jason Jones, Ian Hilditch, Simon Hillman, Tat Wa Lay, Grant Lock, Tony Honeker, Neil Partridge, David Pearson, Vai On Ho, Aiden White, Jason Weeks, Hywel Price Evans, Becky Hart, Jo Whittington, Lisa Winstone, Susan Cazenove, Barbara Fadden, Victoria George, Samantha Harding, Sarah Vaughton, Laura Jones, Darpan Kaur, Sally Martin, Sabrina Morris, Natasha Motee, Arabella Hartland Peel, Sousila Pillay, Toni Rice, Sukhi Kaur, Jillian Wildgoose ....Guests

Ben Fido, Mike Smith, Hilary Morris, Muriel Smith .... Older Guest

Sarah Wright, Lisa Unique, Charlotte Geen .... Lab Assistants

Charles Jarman ....Stunt Double for Leo Jones

Tracie Simpson, Jennie Fava, Steve Smith ....Horrified Beautiful Guests

Alex and Unknown ....Paramedics

David Bednall ....Hand Double for The Doctor

Chris Islington, Grainne Jougin, Sonal Mamta, Gary Marriott ....Unknown

Nick Wilkes, Vernon Keeble-Watson, Paul Ganney, Emma Feeney, Wendi Sheard, Joanna Campera .... Crowd ADR.

CREDITS

Written by Stephen Greenhorn
Produced by Phil Collinson
Directed by Richard Clark
1st Assistant Director: Dan Mumford
2nd Assistant Director: Jennie Fava [uncredited: Steffan Morris]
3rd Assistant Director: Sarah Davies [uncredited: Fraser Fennell Ball]
Location Manager: Lowri Thomas
Unit Manager: Rhys Griffiths [uncredited: Huw Jones]
Production Co-ordinator: Jess van Niekerk
Production Secretary: Kevin Myers
Production Assistant: Debi Griffiths
Floor Runners: Lowri Denman, Barry Phillips
Contracts Assistant: Kath Blackman
Continuity: Non Eleri Hughes
Script Editor: Simon Winstone
Focus Puller: Steve Rees [uncredited: Marc Covington]
Polecam Operator: Andy Leonard
Grip: John Robinson [uncredited: Clive Baldwin]
Camera Assistant: Penny Shipton
Boom Operators: Jon Thomas, Bryn Thomas

[uncredited: Kevin Staples]

Gaffer: Mark Hutchings [uncredited: Steve Slocombe]

Best Boy: Peter Chester

Stunt Co-ordinators: Tom Lucy

Stunt Performers: Charles Jarman

Chief Supervising Art Director: Stephen Nicholas

Art Dept Production Manager: Jonathan
 Marquand Allison

Art Dept Co-ordinator: Matthew North

Chief Props Master: Adrian Anscombe

Supervising Art Director: Arwel Wyn Jones

Associate Designer: James North

Set Decorator: Malin Lindholm

Standby Art Director: Leonie Rintler

Design Assistants: Peter McKinstry, Ben Austin

Cyfle Trainee: Naseem Syed

Standby Props: Phil Shellard, Nick Murray

Standby Carpenter: Paul Jones

Standby Painter: Ellen Woods

Standby Rigger: Bryan Griffiths [uncredited: Ian
 Redmond, Carl Lockyer]

Property Master: Paul Aitken

Props Buyer: Blaanid Maddrell

Chief Props Maker: Barry Jones

Props Makers: Penny Howarth, Mark Cordory,
 Nick Robatto

Construction Manager: Matthew Hywel-Davies

Construction Chargehand: Allen Jones

Graphics: BBC Wales Graphics

Assistant Costume Designer: Marnie Ormiston

Costume Supervisor: Lindsay Bonaccorsi

Costume Assistants: Sheenagh O'Marah,
 Kirsty Wilkinson [uncredited: Angela Jones,
 Ian Chapman, Ali Kedge, Rose Goodhart, John Laurie]

Make-Up Artists: Pam Mullins, Steve Smith,
 John Munro [uncredited: Ros Wilkins, Julie Davies,
 Sara Anghard]

Special Effects Co-ordinator: Ben Ashmore

Special Effects Supervisor: Paul Kelly

Special Effects Technicians: Danny Hargreaves,
 Henry Brook: [uncredited: Mike Crowley]

Prosthetics Designer: Neill Gorton

Prosthetics Supervisor: Rob Mayor

Prosthetics Technician: Helen Rowe, Alex Wothey

Casting Associate: Andy Brierley

VFX Editor: Ceres Doyle

Assistant Editor: Tim Hodges

Post Production Supervisors: Samantha Hall,
 Chris Blatchford

Post Production Co-ordinator: Marie Brown

On Line Editor: Matthew Clarke

Colourist: Mick Vincent

3D Artists: Nicolas Hernandez, Jean-Claude Deguara,
 Neil Roche, Jean Yves Audouard, Jeff North

2D Artists: Sara Bennett, Melissa Butler-Adams, Tim
 Barter, Greg Spencer, Adam Rowland, Bryan Bartlett

Visual Effects Co-ordinators: Jenna Powell,
 Rebecca Johnson

Digital Matte Painters: Simon Wicker, Charlie Bennett

On Set VFX Supervisor: Barney Curnow

Dubbing Mixer: Tim Ricketts

Supervising Sound Editor: Paul McFadden

Sound Editor: Doug Sinclair

Sound FX Editor: Paul Jefferies

Foley Editor: Kelly-Marie Angell

Finance Manager: Chris Rogers

With thanks to the BBC National Orchestra of Wales

Original Theme Music: Ron Grainer

Casting Director: Andy Pryor CDG

Production Executive: Julie Scott

Production Accountant: Endaf Emyr Williams

Sound Recordist: Julian Howarth
 [uncredited: Ray Parker]

Costume Designer: Louise Page

Make-Up Designer: Barbara Southcott

Music: Murray Gold

Visual Effects: The Mill

Visual FX Producers: Will Cohen, Marie Jones

Visual FX Supervisor: Dave Houghton

Special Effects: Any Effects

Prosthetics: Millennium FX

Editor: John Richards

Production Designer: Edward Thomas

Director of Photography: Rory Taylor

Production Manager: Tracie Simpson [uncredited:
 Debbi Slater]

Executive Producers: Russell T Davies, Julie Gardner

BBC Wales in association with the Canadian
Broadcasting Corporation

© MMVII

Profile

ADJOA ANDOH
Francine Jones

"Keep away from my daughter!"

Opposite:
Adjoa Andoh as the outspoken mother of Martha Jones.

Adjoa Andoh (Adjoa being Ghanaian for 'Monday') became a household name with soap fans after three series of BBC medical drama *Casualty*, in which she played Staff Nurse (later Sister) Colette Griffiths in almost 100 episodes between 2000 and 2003. Yet despite this mainstream profile, Andoh had learned her craft within radical black and feminist theatre circles in the 80s.

Andoh was born on 14 January 1962 in Bristol. Her mother was a white English teacher of History and Modern Dance, while her father had been a journalist and folk musician in his native Ghana. Her performing parents encouraged her to put on plays with friends and neighbours, giving her the acting bug young. The family moved to a tiny village in the Cotswolds, where she found that she, her brother and father were the only black faces: "I had to learn to fight pretty quickly at school," she later recalled.

The battles for acceptance saw Andoh drawn to the outsider music of the original punk rock in the late 70s and she hoped to play bass guitar in a punk band, but while studying law at Bristol Polytechnic she became more engaged in political activism (marching to Greenham Common to protest against nuclear weapons) and a black women's group. It was through this collective that she successfully auditioned for a play funded by the Left-leaning Greater London Council.

Numerous roles in radical fringe theatre followed, but a decade or so later her stage reputation had grown so considerably that she was performing with the country's most prestigious theatre groups, including the Royal Court, the National Theatre and the Royal Shakespeare Company, playing everyone from Medea to Condoleezza Rice along the way.

On TV, entry-level roles included one-off parts in *EastEnders*, *The Bill* and a single episode of *Casualty* in 1993. An early break came in the BBC's medical sitcom *Health and Efficiency* where she played Sister Beth Williams over two series in 1993-95. Fantasy fans may recall her appearing in the revived series of *The Tomorrow People: The Rameses Connection* (1995).

Crime drama would provide steady TV work, with parts in the *Jonathan Creek* episode *The Curious Tale of Mr Spearfish* (1999), *Dalziel and Pascoe* (2005), *Wire in the Blood* (2007), *Silent Witness* (2007) and more

recently a regular role in *Law and Order: UK* (2011-14).

Andoh appeared behind the cat make-up of Sister Jatt in *New Earth* [2006 – see Volume 51] before appearing regularly as Martha's mother Francine throughout the 2007 series of *Doctor Who* (and reprising the part for 2008's finale *Journey's End*). She highly rated the programme's showrunner Russell T Davies: "All the wonderful actors that this country has are banging on the door to be in it, I've had a fantastic time doing it… and why are we all attracted to it? Why do we all want to watch it? Because the writing is so fabulous. When the material is *that* good, you're always going to have something that people want to be in, want to work on and want to watch."

Younger fans of fantasy adventure would know Andoh as the head of MI9 in spy series *MI High* (2008-11) and as Old Bethesta in *Wizards vs Aliens* (2014).

She has made a few appearances in movies in recent years, including Clint Eastwood's *Invictus* (2009), a biopic of Nelson Mandela in which Andoh played Mandela's chief of staff, Brenda Maziubo. She also starred in *Adulthood* (2008) written and directed by, and starring, *Doctor Who's* Noel Clarke.

Her most recent TV appearance was in the second series of David Tennant's crime drama serial *Broadchurch* (2015) and she provided the voice of Colonel Casey in *Thunderbirds Are Go!* ∎

42

> STORY 184

Trapped on a spaceship that is on a collision
course with a sun, the Doctor and Martha
have just 42 minutes to save the ship, its
crew and themselves, as well as to defeat an
alien entity that wants everyone to burn.

Introduction

On a purely superficial level, *42* is one of those stories where everything seems to have fallen into place. The title is a witty reversal of US drama series *24* – the obvious touchstone for writer Chris Chibnall when asked to write an episode that occurs in real-time (*24* centring on the gimmick of being 24 hour-long episodes that tell the events of one day). Moreover, 42 is also the rough duration of the episode they were making. This meant that Chibnall could turn the vaguest of starting points into a celebration of one of the series' most enduring dramatic devices...

Countdowns have always been a part of *Doctor Who*: from one of the earliest examples – the Daleks counting down the rels to the detonation of their neutron bomb in the series' second-ever story –

through the 66-second death sentence seen in *Mummy on the Orient Express* [2014 – see Volume 78] and off into the future. Every Doctor has faced a countdown of one sort or another. Even the Eighth Doctor in his sole outing [1996 – see Volume 47] faced a race against the clock.

The whole of *42* is one long countdown. The Doctor has 42 minutes to stop the stricken mining ship *SS Pentallian* from plunging into a nearby sun. He has to uncover what's impeding the ship's engines, rescue his companion from a fiery death and answer some ill-timed pub-quiz trivia. The jeopardy is compounded by there being no way out. The second they land, the Doctor and Martha are isolated from the TARDIS. They find themselves on a vessel, somewhere in deep space, with no hope of rescue. The tension builds; the minutes and seconds tick their way down towards almost certain death...

In the years following *42*'s broadcast, flashbacks and time-bending plot devices became more common and, by comparison, its straightforward approach seems refreshingly simple. There are certainly earlier examples of stories that, pretty much, happen in real-time. A few short months into the first series, *Inside the Spaceship* [1964 – see Volume 2] told a story set in the TARDIS which unfolds in a fairly sequential manner – breaking only once, in the middle. But no one had previously made an episode with the *intention* of telling a story in that fashion.

Part of *Doctor Who*'s appeal is escapism; the opportunity to share in the adventures of the Doctor and his companion. Here, we're with them every step of the way... ∎

'THE TENSION BUILDS; THE MINUTES AND SECONDS TICK THEIR WAY DOWN TOWARDS ALMOST CERTAIN DEATH...'

STORY

Answering a distress signal, the TARDIS lands in a steaming vent chamber. The Doctor and Martha emerge and step through a bulkhead door. Three people race towards them, McDonnell, Scannell and Vashtee, and seal the door. They are on a spaceship, the engines are dead, and in 42 minutes it will crash into a sun! [1]

The engines were sabotaged by one of the crew. The Doctor notices that the ship uses fusion scoops. He asks about the auxiliary engines and is told they are at the front of the ship – but to get there you need to pass through 29 password-protected doors. Martha and Vashtee set off.

In the medi-bay two of the crew, Ashton and Lerner, restrain a third, Korwin, McDonnell's husband. The Doctor sedates him and tells Lerner to perform a bio-scan. [2]

Martha and Vashtee make it through two doors, thanks to the Doctor's knowledge of happy primes. The third door's password is a question; who had the most pre-download number ones, Elvis or the Beatles? Martha phones her mother who looks up the answer on the internet; it's Elvis.

Lerner contacts the Doctor. Korwin's biological make-up is changing. Korwin walks up to her, repeats "Burn with me!" and opens his eyes. There is a blinding glare and Lerner is vapourised. [3]

The Doctor tells McDonnell that Korwin has been taken over, cannot be cured, and must be stopped before he kills again. The Doctor is correct and it isn't long before, Korwin (now wearing a welding mask) kills another crew member, Erina, and infects Ashton. [4]

Ashton (who is also wearing a mask) catches up with Martha and Vashtee. They hide from him in an escape pod, but Ashton finds them and initiates the jettison programme.

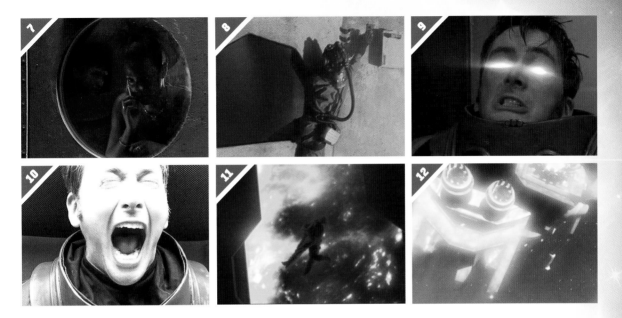

Korwin finds McDonnell and tells her, "It's your fault." [5] Scannell freezes him using an ice vent.

Ashton leaves the Doctor at the airlock as the escape pod is jettisoned. [6]

The Doctor calls Scannell, telling him to bring him a spacesuit. McDonnell discovers Ashton in the medi-bay and shoves him into the stasis chamber, lowering the temperature to kill him.

Scannell provides the Doctor with a spacesuit. The Doctor intends to boost the magnetic lock on the ship's exterior to attract the escape pod.

Martha calls her mother to tell her she loves her, her father, Leo and Tish. [7]

The Doctor climbs out into space and reaches the lever to remagnetise the pod. [8] Back in the airlock, he looks at the sun and realises it is alive. The pod returns but Martha finds the Doctor crawling on the ground. He has become infected! [9]

He explains that when the ship scooped the sun's surface for fuel they took its heart. He tells Martha he must be frozen or it will force him to kill her. Martha takes him to the medi-bay, places him in the stasis chamber and starts to freeze him. [10] But the power is cut from engineering by Korwin, who is still alive.

The Doctor tells Martha to vent the engines. Meanwhile, Scannell and Vashtee unlock the last of the password doors. McDonnell finds Korwin and lures him into an airlock. Once inside, she opens the exterior door and they are sucked out into space. [11]

Scannell and Vashtee reach the auxiliary engines. Martha joins them and tells them to dump the fuel. They do so and the engines start working again using the reserves. [12]

The Doctor recovers and later he and Martha say goodbye to Scannell and Vashtee. In the TARDIS, the Doctor gives Martha a key. She receives a call from her mother, inviting her to come round. It's Election Day. But Francine is not alone – two of Saxon's agents are listening in…

Pre-production

"Maybe you'd like to do an episode of the 2008 series of *Doctor Who?"* asked Julie Gardner in a text to Chris Chibnall, co-producer and main writer on *Torchwood,* in July 2006. At the time, Chibnall had just written the script for the *Torchwood* episode *Cyberwoman,* was on paternity leave, and had to consider how to schedule this offer alongside his commitments to *Torchwood.*

A fan of *Doctor Who* during its original run, Chris Chibnall had contributed to fanzines and had also featured on an edition of BBC1's *Open Air* commenting on *The Trial of a Time Lord* [1986 – see Volume 42] on Monday 8 December 1986. After studying Drama and English at St Mary's College Twickenham, Chibnall worked at Sky and then undertook further study for an MA in Theatre and Film at Sheffield University before working in the theatre and writing plays. His first TV credit was on the 2001 revival of *Crossroads,* following on from which he co-created the rural series *Born and Bred* for BBC One in 2002. Having worked with Julie Gardner before on a development project, Chris met the executive producer again in August 2005 when she offered him a chance to work on the post-watershed *Doctor Who* spin-off, *Torchwood;* at the same time, the writer was also penning an episode for *Life on Mars.*

Below:
The Doctor and McDonnell realise that something deadly is on the prowl aboard the ship.

During a tone meeting on *Torchwood*, Chris grabbed the chance to talk to Russell T Davies and Julie Gardner about their proposal. The original idea put forward at the first story meeting by Davies during summer 2006 was very different to the eventual story, and far more expensive. During the subsequent period when Chibnall was writing *End of Days*, the finale of *Torchwood*'s first series, the requirement for *Doctor Who* changed and was now outlined by Davies as: "Spaceship, sun, glowing eyes and a spacewalk."

Chibnall was surprised to be given an episode set in space. Having established the episode's setting as a spacestation, there was a fleeting suggestion that the narrative would be set in the same future as the previous series' *The Impossible Planet/ The Satan Pit* [2006 – see Volume 53], and for a couple of days the team considered that the hold of the ship could contain Ood, which would cover Russell's concern that the episode did not have a traditional monster. However, this was dropped even before the story reached a first draft.

Real-time

To familiarise himself with the character of Martha, Chris read some of the scripts already written; this was one of the last scripts to go into development for the 2007 series and as such Russell had already planned out the concluding episodes of the run and Chris was able to read the scripts for *Human Nature/The Family of Blood* [2007 – see Volume 56]. Chris told *Doctor Who Magazine* that in his first outline, "I suggested that the ship was a research facility, which had been studying the sun for generations. Russell pointed out that such a back-story would take too long to explain." In addition to the fact that after 200 years,

Above: Martha has faith that the Doctor will save the day.

the scientists hadn't figured out that the sun they were studying was alive, Russell's concerns were that the spacestation setting lacked the potential to be dynamic, and felt that a spaceship setting would be better; this was something that the series had not attempted since its return in 2005. By now, Chris had completed *End of Days* and – having submitted his story breakdown for his *Doctor Who* episode – had fallen down the stairs at home. Lying flat on his back at home, he took a conference call from Russell and Julie who outlined the proposed changes and Russell also identified a key gimmick for the episode. "He said, 'Tell you what: they've just got there and let's do it in real-time'," recalled the writer in *Doctor Who Magazine*. Chris admired this aspect of the US thriller series *24* and enjoyed the challenge of telling a *Doctor Who* story in this way with Russell suggesting that his script could have "at least 20 pages of running up and down corridors". Chibnall noted that this move freed him from over-intellectualising the story and turned it into a straight thriller, offering the added element of the viewer sharing every second of the tension with

Connections:
Freeze it out of me

▶ The Doctor told Martha that he could withstand a temperature of 200 degrees below zero, having survived a freezing process; he had survived "several hundred degrees" below freezing by the Moroks in the story *The Space Museum* [1965 – see Volume 5].

the characters; as such he came up with the element of pub quiz-style questions to open the vital bulkhead doors that the crew needed to pass through. "Real-time is just an easy thing for people to understand, and it gives you a hook," the writer told *Doctor Who Magazine*, "The moment it was mentioned that this would be a 42-minute real-time episode, Russell said, 'That's the title: *42*!'" Chris Chibnall liked this as it was also a playful reference to the number defined as the Answer to the Ultimate Question of Life, the Universe and Everything in the 1978 radio series *The Hitchhiker's Guide to the Galaxy* written by one-time *Doctor Who* script editor Douglas Adams.

When envisaging the spaceship for his script, Chris thought a great deal about the style and texture of the vehicle, seeing it as dirty like an industrial lorry, and manned by a crew which was there simply to earn a living rather than for

the glory of travelling in space. The ship was initially named the *SS Icarus* after the figure from Greek mythology who fell to his death when he flew too near the sun and the heat melted the wax binding the feathered wings strapped to his arms; this name was suggested by script editor Simon Winstone. Of the crew, Ashton was originally called Motta, but this name was changed because it sounded too similar to 'Martha'. Riley was named after Chris Chibnall's godson, and Davies originally wanted the character to be called Riley Kincade, but then used Kincade as part of Brannigan's full name in his own script for *Gridlock* [2007 – see page 17]. Chibnall was also keen to employ elements of bodily possession and characters hiding behind masks. The use of the industrial visors was partially inspired by the character of the superhero Cyclops who could produce optic blasts from his eyes (forcing him to wear a visor), who had débuted in the first issue of Marvel Comics' *X-Men* in 1963; it was also a practical element to stop the infected characters burning everything that they looked at.

"In a way this is Martha's first story as a proper companion," commented Davies on *Doctor Who Confidential*. With the Doctor partially incapacitated and requiring the help of Martha, the story was to see the Doctor fully accepting his new acquaintance as a travelling companion, and Chris was asked to make her a major part of his narrative. A key sequence was the launch of the escape pod, with the Doctor screaming "I'll save you" to Martha being inspired by the sequence of Hawkeye promising "I will find you" to Cora in the 1992 movie *The Last of the Mohicans*. Chris had originally considered having Martha infected by the force of the sun, and when asking Russell if he could do this was urged to go further and infect the Doctor instead.

Below:
Scannell works to kick-start the ship's engines.

A veteran director of *Doctor Who* since 1983, Harper had directed two of the three two-part stories in the 2006 series, since when he had been working on BBC One's *Robin Hood* in Hungary.

The tone meeting for the episode was held at Upper Boat on the morning of Monday 11 December – only hours after the *Doctor Who* Christmas party for cast and crew had concluded. Comparing the episode to *The Satan Pit*, Russell specified the defining word for the instalment as "hot!", with Harper considering how best to employ the use of a tricky heat haze effect. When production designer Edward Thomas was concerned about the engine of the *SS Icarus*, described in the script as a 'dirty huge cylindrical tank, spinning like a cement mixer chugging away', this was quickly dropped to save on design elements. Harper was aware that since the precise timings of events would not be known until the edit, the episode would be made without any countdown clocks in shot, and that the countdown and computer voice would be added in post-production to fit the edited programme.

Left:
The Doctor instructs Abi Lerner to lower Korwin's body temperature.

After a story meeting for the second series of *Torchwood* on Wednesday 25 October, Davies asked Chibnall to add in some new material with Martha's mother, Francine, and a sinister agent of Mr Saxon who had been added at short notice to the script of *The Lazarus Experiment* [2007 – see page 89] (as 'Mysterious Man') a couple of weeks earlier; this was an opportunity for Davies to seed another element which would lead towards the climax of the series. The idea of McDonnell's self-sacrifice at the end of the episode came from Julie Gardner. In early drafts, McDonnell had lured the infected Korwin into the airlock to dispose of him, and although Russell T Davies was uneasy about this concept initially, the story was structured so that ultimately McDonnell had no other choice.

It was decided that, along with Russell T Davies' script for *Utopia* [2007 – see Volume 56], *42* would form the seventh production block of the series, to be directed in early 2007 by Graeme Harper.

Freezing temperatures

The script originally had the Doctor performing a spacewalk along the length of the *Icarus* to reach the flight deck, which Davies wanted to feel like "mountaineering inside a furnace". However, since the original conception of the storyline, the budget had been drastically reduced; during the planning meetings it was felt that this would be too time-consuming on the special effects requirements. "We just couldn't achieve it in terms of the number of special effects shots it would have needed to sell it, so we asked Chris to have a think about how he might scale it down," explained producer Phil Collinson on *42*'s podcast commentary. Chibnall amended this instead to the sequence of the Doctor trying to reach a vital lever situated outside the ship's airlock. This also gave a key element to the presentation of the Doctor as Russell told *Doctor Who Confidential*: "He's going to be a hero. He's going to physically risk his life… He's got to expose himself to the sun. He's got to be reaching for a button that is out of reach."

The original plan was that *42* would be recorded first, followed by *Utopia*. However, in mid-December just before the Christmas break, the decision was taken to kick off Block Seven with *Utopia* instead.

Following Christmas, another tone meeting was held at Upper Boat on the morning of Wednesday 3 January 2007, by which time a location venue had been found for the *SS Icarus*' engineering room and central corridor in the form of a disused paper mill in Caldicot owned by the St Regis Paper Company. The main concern now was that in the freezing January atmosphere, the breath of the actors might be visible – not quite right for a ship minutes from being engulfed by a fiery sun!

Below: Korwin struggles against his possession.

On Friday 5 January, the plan for Block Seven was changed again, and at short notice it was decided that *42* would enter production ahead of *Utopia* due to scheduling issues with *Utopia*'s guest star, Sir Derek Jacobi. The design team rose to the occasion and rescheduled their work to construct the interiors of the *Icarus* sooner than expected. Costume designer Louise Page had only two days to source the costumes for the ship's crew, and went for the look of combat vest and tops inspired by the 1979 sci-fi thriller movie *Alien*. It was decided that visually the episode would be set in the same timeframe as *The Impossible Planet/The Satan Pit*.

Voiceless

A technical recce for the block was held on Tuesday 9 and Wednesday 10 January. In Chibnall's draft scripts, the *SS Icarus* was originally in the Peony System – named after the colourful, fragrant flower – but this was altered to the Toraji System before the readthrough when it was realised that 'Peony' sounded uncomfortably similar to 'penis'.

The readthrough for *42* and *Utopia* took place on the morning of Thursday 11 January at Upper Boat, and with David Tennant having lost his voice, script editor and former actor Gary Russell stood in as the Doctor at this initial reading. Just back from holiday in Bali, the main guest artiste for the episode was Michelle Collins, best known as Cindy Beale in the BBC One soap opera *EastEnders*. Cast as McDonnell, Collins had previously worked on *Sea of Souls* with producer Phil Collinson. Great pains were taken to try to keep the casts of the two episodes apart so that the revelation of the Master's return in *Utopia* would not leak out. A production meeting was held for *42* that afternoon.

'THE SCRIPT ORIGINALLY HAD THE DOCTOR PERFORMING A SPACEWALK ALONG THE LENGTH OF THE ICARUS.'

The shooting script for *42* was issued on Friday 12 January. As with Rose before her in *The End of the World* [2005 – see Volume 48], the Doctor was able to modify Martha's mobile so that she could phone home (although on this occasion he did this using the sonic screwdriver rather than installing a device as he had for Rose); when leaving the TARDIS, the Doctor originally said, "Come on, Martha Jones! No dawdling!" This was replaced in the ADR script because Davies felt it sounded too much like the Doctor of the first six episodes of this series, not the Doctor who'd now accepted Martha as his companion. The spaceship's central corridor was described as a 'sweaty, greasy, industrial cargo vessel' while the exterior was a 'bulky old tramp steamer of a spaceship'. The crew of the ship comprised Kath McDonnell, described as 'female, early 30s, sexy, smart, rough edges', Orin Scannell who was 'male, early 30s, mouthy hothead', Riley Vashtee who was 'sexy, blokey, early 20s', while Erina Lissak (later changed to Lessak) was '19,

sure of herself, clad in welding gear and helmet', Korwin McDonnell was 'tall, well-built, early 30s', Dev Ashton was 'male, 50s, tired, his last tour' and Abi Lerner was 'female, mid-20s, doctor; green scrubs'.

When the first computer announcement of impact projection was given, McDonnell said, "Ignore it. It's what computers do!" It was noted of the comms pads on the ship that they were numeric keypads marked 0-9 plus buttons marked MED, ENG, HOLD, AUX and ALL. When calling Korwin on the Comms, McDonnell originally tried to reassure herself by saying, "They're probably sorting things out. I'm sure they're fine."

One of the password questions related to singer Elvis Presley and the 1960s band The Beatles, with the Doctor saying, *"Here Comes the Sun"*, the title of a song from The Beatles' 1969 album *Abbey Road* and also considering the JXL remix of Presley's *A Little Less Conversation* which topped the charts in June 2002 (something raised

Right:
Martha is horrified to discover that they are falling into a sun.

by brand manager Edward Russell at the episode's readthrough). Francine's answer to Martha was originally more detailed: "[Elvis] had eighteen, Beatles had seventeen." When Korwin advanced on Lerner in the medi-bay, she originally observed, "You shouldn't be up! You've had enough trank to knock out a horse." When Korwin opened his eyes, the script noted, 'dazzling, bright white light shines from them. (Dazzling glow, not a directional beam)'. When he left the medi-bay, the script noted that Korwin was 'strong, fast, implacable. (Never running, purposeful, scary striding like Robert Patrick in *Terminator 2*)', making a comparison to the 1991 science-fiction thriller *Terminator 2: Judgment Day* in which Patrick played the T-1000 cyborg. The phrase "burn with me!" was crafted as a catchphrase akin to the memorable "are you my mummy?" from the 2005 story *The Empty Child/The Doctor Dances* [see Volume 50].

Countdown

The Sierpinski sequence was named after the Polish mathematician Waclaw Sierpinski who came up with many numeric theories. When Ashton was lured to the medi-bay from the central corridor, he originally heard a loud wolf whistle from McDonnell.

Listening in on Francine Jones' calls to Martha was the 'Sinister Man from *The Lazarus Experiment*'. After the Doctor was possessed by the life force of the sun, McDonnell said, "I'm sorry! I didn't know." "Give back what you took," retorted the Doctor. This was later changed to dialogue about the fusion scoops being illegal. Speaking to Martha before he was to be frozen, the Doctor made reference to the process of regeneration.

A late addition to the shooting script was the Doctor giving Martha a key to the TARDIS; this was at the behest of Russell T Davies who knew that he needed her to have a key in his scripts for *The Sound of Drums* and *Last of the Time Lords* [2007 – see Volume 56]

The original chronology for the main events was that the initial impact projection was 42 minutes 15 seconds, with the opening credits starting as the clock reached 42:00. The Doctor made for engineering at 40:19, went up to the medi-bay at 37:57 and left at 35:05, and his realisation of how to jump start the engines was at 31:19. Martha phoned Francine at 29:29, Lerner's screams were heard at 27:11, Erina was killed at 25:32, the escape pod was launched at 18:22 and Martha said goodbye to her mum at 13:43. The Doctor was rushed to the medi-bay at 7:07 and McDonnell hurried to engineering at 3:28. The final sequence as the TARDIS departed was set 'a few hours later.' ■

Connections: Undefeated

❱ The Doctor urged Scannell not to give in and asked ,"Where's your Dunkirk spirit?" in reference to the defiant attitude displayed by Britain in managing to evacuate its stranded forces from France in May/June 1940.

Above: Erina falls victim to the sun entity.

Production

Recording on Block Seven began at Upper Boat on Monday 15 January with work on the TARDIS set for first *Utopia* and then *42*. The escape pod set had been quickly constructed – with a cool blue interior contrasting with the fiery red inside the *SS Icarus* – and the scenes of Martha and Riley in the pod with Ashton trying to reach them were recorded after a make-up change for Freema Agyeman; unfortunately the initial make-up used to simulate heat brought the actress out in a rash and so for subsequent sessions she simply used blusher. "The difficulty I had was to make sure that everybody in every scene was giving it pace and energy, remembering the clock is ticking," Graeme Harper told *Doctor Who Confidential*; before each take he would bellow out to his cast, "Loads of pace and energy!" As with most days on the shoot, work ran from 8am to 7pm, and in tandem with the first day's recording, stunt arranger Abbi Collins attended meetings concerning the wire work sequence for the demise of McDonnell and her husband.

Floating in space

David Tennant was not available for recording on the afternoon of Tuesday 16 January when work continued on the escape pod and airlock scenes. At the same time, Abbi Collins worked with wire expert Kevin Welch in preparation for the stunt scene the following day. *Doctor Who Confidential* was present at Upper Boat on Wednesday 17 to cover the scenes with the Doctor climbing out on to the hull of the *SS Icarus* – a very small section of the ship's exterior. "It was one of the most exhausting sequences I've done on the show, and that's saying something to be honest," David Tennant told *Doctor Who Confidential* about this sequence. Following this, the scenes with McDonnell in the airlock with her possessed husband were recorded; when the pair were sucked out into space, the actors were yanked out of the airlock set on hip harnesses and landed on crash mats. Following this, the actors recorded a shot of the McDonnells together floating in space, suspended on wires against a greenscreen – a scene which was originally to be filmed on 16mm film rather than captured on videotape. This was Michelle Collins' first work on the episode, having spent the morning rehearsing the wire sequence with Matthew Chambers. "That was all very difficult. First day of filming. First day nerves. And you've got stuntmen," the actress told *Doctor Who Confidential*, then adding of being suspended on wires against a greenscreen, "I quite liked being up there actually. It was quite liberating… But I couldn't stay up too long." For his performance as the possessed Korwin, Chambers had in mind not only the T-1000 indicated in the script, but also the lead character from the 1987 science-fiction action movie *RoboCop*. Around this work, a pick-up unit was recording insert shots on the TARDIS set for *Human Nature* with David and Freema, along with an insert needed for *Smith and Jones* [2007 – see Volume 54].

Under the eye of *Doctor Who Confidential*, the *Doctor Who* team began work at the

'FOR HIS PERFORMANCE AS THE POSSESSED KORWIN, CHAMBERS HAD IN MIND ROBOCOP.'

St Regis Paper Company on Thursday 18, recording in the engineering section of the ship located beneath the rollers in the grimy paper mill, the BBC design crew having dressed the area with comms devices and control panels, some of which were taken from stock. "We used a lot of yellow, to suggest light from the sun," Edward Thomas told *Doctor Who Magazine*, "I also hammered home the colour red... fire engines are red, and when you think of those, you naturally think 'fire'." The oily locations were dressed in shades of hot steamy orange and amber to enhance the stifling atmosphere. The crew wore heavy coats to ward off the freezing conditions, but these could only be donned by the cast between takes; massive heaters blazed away in an attempt to keep the temperatures high. To prevent breath being visible on screen, the cast was offered ice cream to eat or ice cubes to put in their mouths, but most battled on without these aids. To make the characters show the effects of intense heat, the cast members were covered in baby oil and had grease in their hair. "It was very uncomfortable, because baby oil makes you feel really yucky, and I had to have it on my hair and hands, and my hands had to be filthy," Michelle Collins told *Radio Times*. Two camera units were recording, with the engineering scenes covering the early sequences along with the taping of comms voices for other scenes.

Freema was not required for recording at St Regis on Friday 19 when further engineering scenes were recorded, including the luring of Korwin under the cooler vent. For the freezing sequences, a gel was added to the costume of the performer, and crystals were sprinkled on top of this to give an icy, glassy look. A powder was applied on a gel in a similar way for make-up. When Korwin attacked Ashton, Gary Powell – who played Ashton

– had to keep drinking ice-cold water to stop vapour coming out of his mouth, while hidden tubes ran up the sleeves of Matthew Chambers' costume through which were pumped carbon dioxide.

The scenes with the defrosted Korwin were completed on Saturday 20 January, with some other sequences in the central corridor – the long chamber for which St Regis had been an ideal location – being deferred. While Freema Agyeman rejoined the crew, David Tennant was not required and was released for the weekend. The long central corridor was to be re-dressed as each of the chambers that the characters had to pass through on their battle to start the engines, and the first of these sequences to be enacted was Scannell and McDonnell moving along the central corridor and Martha running the length of the ship. Work then continued with the locker area scenes where Korwin confronted Erina.

Over the weekend, the recording schedule was amended. Two scenes scheduled for Monday 22 January at St Regis were those in the ante-room where the TARDIS landed, but these along with material in the storage area were deferred for several days. Instead, scenes planned for the next day were pulled forward with work focusing on Area #30 of the central corridor, starting with the early scenes of the Doctor and Martha meeting the crew. Wrapped up warmly, Chris Chibnall and script editor Simon Winstone visited the mill to watch the two camera units at work and also spoke to David Tennant for his video diary.

Paper mill

Tom Spilsbury, Deputy Editor of *Doctor Who Magazine*, was on location for scenes set in Areas #30 through to #27 on Tuesday 23 January, watching the early sequences of Martha and Riley setting off along the central corridor. The corridor was re-dressed as Area #17 for work on Wednesday 24 which saw the recordings of Martha and Riley being confronted by

Ashton, the Doctor trying to reach Martha and then the first few scenes with the Doctor housing the force of the sun; David Tennant took pleasure in revealing the lighting effects of this material for his video diary. These scenes continued on to Thursday 25, also taking in the sequences of Riley and Scannell moving through Areas #22 and #21, and concluding with the scenes book-ending the main action with the TARDIS in the ante-room. This was part of the paper mill which had required no dressing apart from the addition of the familiar police box and a few machines to generate some steam.

Back at Upper Boat on Friday 26 January, the medi-bay set was now completed; this was an operational set with the sliding couch of the stasis chamber – a

Connections: Driving force

❯ The eventual name of the ship, *SS Pentallian*, was a corruption of the Pentalion drive, part of the transmat in the 1975 serial *Revenge of the Cybermen* [see Volume 23].

Below: Director Graeme Harper prepares to record a scene.

Above left:
It's all McDonnell's fault!

Above right:
Engineer Dev Ashton won't survive the day.

re-dress of the MRI machine from *Smith and Jones* – which could not be built on location. The first day covered the early scenes with Korwin being tended to. Two cameras were used, with a third crew from *Doctor Who Confidential* on hand and events also being viewed by Jason Arnopp of *Doctor Who Magazine*.

After the weekend, *Doctor Who Confidential* covered more medi-bay scenes on Monday 29 January. In these scenes, Korwin killed Lerner, McDonnell punched Ashton, and the Doctor was frozen in stasis (with the *Doctor Who Confidential* crew eavesdropping on David Tennant's frosty make-up session which the actor also covered in his video diary). This was Michelle Collins' final day on set, following which she became ill as result of the extreme temperatures which she had experienced since her return from Bali.

The final major day of production on *42* was Tuesday 30 January which began with the last few scenes of the Doctor and Martha in the medi-bay at Upper Boat. These were important scenes for the two regular cast members, with Freema commenting to *Doctor Who Confidential* that Martha "needs to think fast and that's the moment where they have the shift in their relationship. [The Doctor] needs her. He's genuinely scared." Following this, the crew travelled to the NEG glass site used on various occasions since work on *Daleks in Manhattan/Evolution of the Daleks* [2007 – see page 60] back in late October. This time, the derelict building became the control wall where Martha, Riley and Scannell would vent the engines and save the *Icarus* from destruction in the closing moments of the episode, after which sequences were also recorded for *Utopia*, with *Doctor Who Confidential* again covering work this day.

Later on in Block Seven, insert shots were recorded for *42* at Upper Boat.

Connections: Space fashions

▶ The spacesuit worn by the Doctor was the same one David Tennant had worn in *The Impossible Planet/ The Satan Pit* [2006 – see Volume 53], but now dyed red instead of orange and with a completely new neck-piece.

On Thursday 8 February, a greenscreen unit worked alongside the main unit on *Utopia* and also recorded a low angle shot of Korwin in the airlock (with a double standing in for Matthew Chambers), a tracking shot of the Doctor and Martha looking out of the portal and a shot of Ashton's hand operating a panel. The following day, a second unit worked on further inserts without any cast, focusing mainly on the consoles and computer screen images seen aboard the *SS Icarus* and the TARDIS, as well as material for the fuel dumping.

Sinister Woman

Further pick-up material was recorded in tandem with Block Eight. On Tuesday 20 February, work for the day began with TARDIS material for *Utopia* at Upper Boat and then moved to a house in Penarth where the scenes with Adjoa Andoh as Francine Jones were recorded amidst her scheduled work for *The Sound of Drums/Last of the Time Lords* [2007 – see Volume 56]; this house was different to the one seen in *Smith and Jones*. By now the 'Sinister Man' of *42* had become a new character, 'Sinister Woman'; in fact this would be a character from *The Sound of Drums* played by Elize du Toit. This change came about as Bertie Carvel, who had played *The Lazarus Experiment*'s 'Mysterious Man', became unavailable. Further pick-ups were performed at base on Thursday 1 March for inserts such as McDonnell's hand hitting the airlock button, the full 45-minute countdown clock and the deadlock questions appearing on the monitor. Director Colin Teague recorded an insert along with his work on *Last of the Time Lords* on Tuesday 6 March showing Erina's hand pressing a button, while the computer screen graphics for the episode were recorded on Tuesday 13 March, again at Upper Boat alongside work for the series' climax. ∎

PRODUCTION

Mon 15 Jan 07 Upper Boat Studios, Trefforest (TARDIS; Spaceship – Airlock/Escape Pod)

Tue 16 Jan 07 Upper Boat Studios (Spaceship – Escape Pod/Airlock)

Wed 17 Jan 07 Upper Boat Studios (Spaceship – Airlock/Airlock #2; Greenscreen)

Thu 18 Jan 07 St Regis Paper Company, Sudbrook Mill, Caldicot, Monmouthshire (Spaceship – Engineering)

Fri 19 Jan 07 St Regis Paper Company (Spaceship – Engineering)

Sat 20 Jan 07 St Regis Paper Company (Spaceship – Engineering/Central Corridor Area #11/#10/#7/#6/#4/#2/Locker Area)

Mon 22 Jan 07 St Regis Paper Company (Spaceship – Central Corridor Area #30)

Tue 23 Jan 07 St Regis Paper Company (Spaceship – Central Corridor Area #30/#29/#28/#27)

Wed 24 Jan 07 St Regis Paper Company (Spaceship – Central Corridor Area #17)

Thu 25 Jan 07 St Regis Paper Company (Spaceship – Central Corridor Area #22/#21/Ante Room)

Fri 26 Jan 07 Upper Boat Studios (Spaceship – Medi-bay)

Mon 29 Jan 07 Upper Boat Studios (Spaceship – Medi-bay)

Tue 30 Jan 07 Upper Boat Studios (Spaceship – Medcentre); Old NEG glass site, Trident Park, Glass Avenue, Cardiff Bay (Spaceship – Control Wall)

Thu 8 Feb 07 Upper Boat Studios (Spaceship – Airlock/Porthole/Central Corridor Area #17)

Fri 9 Feb 07 Upper Boat Studios (Spaceship – Engineering; TARDIS; Spaceship – Central Corridor Area #30/#29/#28/ Control Wall)

Tue 20 Feb 07 Cwrt-y-Vil Road, Penarth (Francine Jones' House – Lounge)

Thu 1 Mar 07 Upper Boat Studios (Spaceship)

Tue 6 Mar 07 Upper Boat Studios (Spaceship)

Tue 13 Mar 07 Upper Boat Studios (Spaceship)

Post-production

Above:
The Doctor is
desperate to
rescue Martha.

It was during February that a glance through the film magazine *Empire* drew Russell T Davies' attention to the major publicity for a new science-fiction movie called *Sunshine* in which the crew of a spaceship had to reignite a dying sun 50 years in the future; he had been aware of the film for a couple of months but decided not to mention it to the rest of the crew. While the actual plot of the film was significantly different to *42*, one aspect which was unfortunately similar was the fact that the spacecraft in *Sunshine* was called the *Icarus II*. With *Sunshine* due to

open at the start of April 2007 in the UK, it was felt prudent to change the name of the vessel in *42*. The new name was the *SS Pentallian*. Fortunately this necessitated minimal dubbing and a change of graphics.

The Mill's CGI contributions to the episode included the *SS Pentallian* itself, some of the interior bulkheads, the various gaseous elements and blazes of light from the eyes of the infected, and the burning menace of the sun; the shot at the end of the pre-credits was the longest effects shot on the series to date.

Editing of the episode ran throughout March. The producer and director credits were shown over the scene of the Doctor, Martha and the crew entering the engineering section; originally the pre-credit sequence had been changed from the script and concluded with Martha's comment, "We're stuck here," but this was changed back to the scripted version in the final dub (this earlier version was sent out to reviewers on DVD). Minor trims were made to the finished programme. After Scannell said the interior of the vent chamber was like lava, McDonnell explained, "The vents regulate onboard temperature. Turn them off, the ship'll burn in seconds." When Scannell found that the engines were burnt out, he added, "I can't get us out of this, Captain!" Explaining what Korwin did to McDonnell, Ashton originally said that he "shut down the engines... It was all I could do to restrain him," and the raving Korwin gasped, "You don't want me to look at you. It's burning me!" before the Doctor employed the sedative.

Name change

The Doctor calling Abi to check on Korwin was originally later in the show, following his idea of jump-starting the ship; in this sequence, as the Doctor postulated harnessing the generator, he added, "Oh! Inertial confinement!" "Everything's burned out," said Scannell. "There's still fuel in the tank," pointed out the Doctor, "we rig the generators, channel the ions and BANG! Enough energy to blast us away." After the Doctor told McDonnell that her husband had gone, Scannell said, "We're a crew. We stick together." When McDonnell forced Ashton into cryofreeze, she originally looked down, traumatised, at the corpse and said, "I'm sorry." While Scannell was talking to the Doctor as he reached for

the lever on the ship's hull, he originally reminded the Doctor, "What'd you call it, Dunkirk spirit?" A short scene in Area #12 was trimmed; "He did it!" exclaimed McDonnell. Pushing the ALL button, Scannell said, "Doctor! Get back in here now! Those shields are gonna buckle any minute!" As the Doctor looked at the sun, Scannell's voice continued, "Doctor! Did you hear me? Doctor! That airlock has to be closed for the pod to be able to dock! Answer me! Are you alright?"

The main change was the ship's rechristening. Originally when Riley read out, "Date of *SS Icarus*' first flight?", Martha commented, "This ship's called the *Icarus*?" "Yeah, why?" said Riley as he typed. "You really should've been on the lookout for this," replied Martha, wryly. Another minor problem solved with dubbing was to qualify the Elvis Presley/Beatles question for the present-day of Francine Jones by adding the footnote that the number ones related to "pre-download", with three Presley re-issues having hit the top spot in 2005.

An online commentary for the episode was recorded by Phil Collinson, Michelle Collins and Anthony Flanagan, who played Scannell. ■

Below: Scannell tries to persuade the Doctor not to venture outside the ship.

'MICHELLE COLLINS WAS
INTERVIEWED ON BBC ONE'S
BREAKFAST ON THURSDAY 17 MAY.'

Publicity

> The casting of Michelle Collins was announced by the BBC on Wednesday 31 January.

> There was a two-week gap between episodes following the transmission of *The Lazarus Experiment* on 5 May. This was due to the broadcast of the annual *Eurovision Song Contest* on BBC One on Saturday 12 May. However, the *Doctor Who* audience had its appetite whetted for the series' return when a preview for *42* was placed on the *bbc.co.uk* website in the form of a written prologue by Joseph Lidster. This covered the three minutes of Erina's life before she met the Doctor and Martha.

> *Burn, Baby, Burn* was the title of Nick Griffiths' *Doctor Who Watch* piece in *Radio Times* with Michelle Collins

commenting on bringing McDonnell to life and Chris Chibnall recalling the show's production. Mark Braxton noted that *42* 'really gets this series cooking' in the *Today's Choices* section of the magazine, with the listing for the episode accompanied by a publicity shot of McDonnell and the TARDIS. Promotion continued with some clips from *42* when Michelle Collins was interviewed on BBC One's *Breakfast* on Thursday 17 May.

Above: Martha phones home.

Left: Scannell survives the ordeal.

Broadcast

▶ *42* performed well in the 7.15pm slot on Saturday 19 May. *42* had been a significant episode for Martha Jones, now fully accepted by the Doctor as a TARDIS traveller. As Freema Agyeman told *Doctor Who Confidential*, "Key to the flat! It's like she's moved in! It's huge!" The episode was repeated the following night on BBC Three at 8pm and again the following Friday at 9pm as usual. The title of the *Doctor Who Confidential* episode which covered the making of *42* was *Space Craft*; the full version aired on BBC Three at 8pm on Saturday 19 May with the *Cutdown* versions placed after the two subsequent repeats.

Right:
The Doctor is determined to save Martha, whatever the risk to himself.

ORIGINAL TRANSMISSION

EPISODE	DATE	TIME	CHANNEL	DURATION	RATING (CHART POSITION)	APPRECIATION INDEX
42	Saturday 19 May 2007	7.15pm-8pm	BBC One	45'23"	7.41M (16th)	85

Merchandise

Left:
The possessed
Korwin is
beyond saving.

A long with *Daleks in Manhattan/Evolution of the Daleks*, and *The Lazarus Experiment* as *Series 3 Volume 2, 42* was initially released on DVD by 2|entertain in June 2007. It was also included in *The Complete Third Series* DVD box set released in November 2007 which featured an optional commentary track by Russell T Davies and Chris Chibnall. Other bonus material included the episode's network trailer, *David Tennant's Video Diary* and the short version of *Doctor Who Confidential*.

A track of music from *42* was included on Silva Screen's CD of *Doctor Who: Original Television Soundtrack: Series 3*, released in November 2007; this track had also featured in *Gridlock*. In September 2009, Character Options released the *Series 3 Figure Set*. One of the three 5" action figures included was Korwin from *42* . ■

Cast and credits

CAST

David Tennant ....The Doctor
Freema Agyeman ....Martha Jones
with
Michelle Collins .... Kath McDonnell
Adjoa Andoh ....Francine Jones
William Ash ....Riley Vashtee
Anthony Flanagan ....Orin Scannell
Matthew Chamber ....Hal Korwin[1]
Gary Powell ....Dev Ashton
Vinette Robinson .... Abi Lerner
Rebecca Oldfield ....Erina Lessak
Elize Du Toit ....Sinister Woman

[1] Error in credits, character name should be Korwin McDonnell

UNCREDITED

Adrian Walker .... Double for Hal Korwin
David Cordingley, Bernie Hodges ....Henchmen
Joshua Hill ....Countdown Voice

CREDITS

Written by Chris Chibnall
Produced by Phil Collinson
Directed by Graeme Harper
1st Assistant Director: Gareth Williams
2nd Assistant Director: Steffan Morris
3rd Assistant Director: Sarah Davies [uncredited: Paul Bennett, Anna Evans, Vicky Wheel]
Location Manager: Gareth Skelding [uncredited: Antonia Grant]
Unit Manager: Rhys Griffiths
Production Co-ordinator: Jess van Niekerk
Production Secretary: Kevin Myers
Production Assistant: Debi Griffiths
Floor Runners: Lowri Denman, Heddi Joy Taylor
Contracts Assistant: Bethan Britton
Continuity: Non Eleri Hughes
Script Editor: Simon Winstone
Camera Operator: Roger Pearce
Focus Puller: Steve Rees
Grip: John Robinson [uncredited: Ron Nicholls]
Boom Operator: Jeff Welch
Gaffer: Mark Hutchings
Best Boy: Peter Chester
Stunt Co-ordinator: Abbi Collins
Wires: Kevin Welch
Chief Supervising Art Director: Stephen Nicholas
Art Dept Production Manager: Jonathan Marquand Allison
Art Dept Co-ordinator: Matthew North
Chief Props Master: Adrian Anscombe
Supervising Art Director: Arwel Wyn Jones
Associate Designer: James North
Set Decorator: Julian Luxton
Standby Art Director: Lee Gammon
Design Assistants: Ian Bunting, Al Roberts, Peter McKinstry
Storyboard Artist: Shaun Williams
Standby Props: Phil Shellard, Nick Murray
Standby Carpenter: Paul Jones

Standby Painter: Ellen Woods
Standby Rigger: Bryan Griffiths
Property Master: Phil Lyons
Props Buyer: Ben Morris
Props Chargehand: Gareth Jeanne
Practical Electrician: Albert James
Construction Manager: Matthew Hywel-Davies
Construction Chargehand: Allen Jones
Graphics: BBC Wales Graphics
Assistant Costume Designer: Marnie Ormiston
Costume Supervisor: Lindsay Bonaccorsi
Costume Assistants: Sheenagh O'Marah,
  Kirsty Wilkinson
Make-Up Artists: Pam Mullins, Steve Smith,
  John Munro
Casting Associates: Andy Brierley, Kirsty Robertson
VFX Editor: Ceres Doyle
Assistant Editor: Tim Hodges
Post-production Supervisors: Samantha Hall,
  Chris Blatchford
Post-production Co-ordinator: Marie Brown
On Line Editor: Matthew Clarke
Colourist: Mick Vincent
3D Artists: Nicolas Hernandez, Jean-Claude
  Deguara, Nick Webber, Andy Guest,
  Serena Cacciato, Will Pryor, Bruce Magroune
2D Artists: Sara Bennett, Russell Horth,
  Bryan Bartlett, Joseph Courtis, Tim Barter,
  Adam Rowland

Visual Effects Co-ordinators: Rebecca Johnson,
  Jenna Powell
On Set VFX Supervisor: Barney Curnow
Dubbing Mixer: Tim Ricketts
Supervising Sound Editor: Paul McFadden
Sound Editor: Doug Sinclair
Sound FX Editor: Paul Jefferies
Finance Manager: Chris Rogers
With thanks to the BBC National Orchestra of Wales
Original Theme Music: Ron Grainer
Casting Director: Andy Pryor CDG
Production Executive: Julie Scott
Production Accountant: Endaf Emyr Williams
Sound Recordist: Ron Bailey
Costume Designer: Louise Page
Make-Up Designer: Barbara Southcott
Music: Murray Gold
Visual Effects: The Mill
Visual FX Producers: Will Cohen, Marie Jones
Visual FX Supervisor: Dave Houghton
Special Effects: Any Effects
Editor: Will Oswald
Production Designer: Edward Thomas
Director of Photography: Ernie Vincze BSC
Production Manager: Patrick Schweitzer
Executive Producers: Russell T Davies, Julie Gardner
BBC Wales in association with the Canadian
Broadcasting Corporation
© MMVII

Profile

MICHELLE COLLINS
Captain Kath McDonnell

Born 28 May 1961, in Hackney, East London, Collins acted in youth theatre as a teenager including the Royal Court's 'Activists' group and Marylebone's Cockpit Theatre before going on to study drama and theatre at 'O' and 'A' Level at Kingsway Princeton College.

A background part making tea in a promo video for the classic 1979 New Wave hit by Squeeze *Up The Junction* saw Collins divert into the pop world. She subsequently became backing singer 'Candide' for retro pop group Mari Wilson and the Wilsations in 1981. Record

Opposite:
Captain of her ship.

Below:
McDonnell struggles to calm her possessed husband.

company pressure saw Mari go solo in 1982, with the group disbanded.

Returning to acting, Collins' first broadcast acting role was in schools' programme *Going To Work* in 1984. Fellow cast member Sandy Ratcliff won a lead part in the BBC's new soap opera *EastEnders*, launched in February 1985, and while Collins auditioned for the part of punk single mum Mary, she lost out when producers decided against a London actress. Roles followed in BBC Welsh drama *Morgan's Boy* (1984), *The Bill*, *Bergerac* and *Screen Two* play *Lucky Sunil*. One breakthrough was ITV sitcom *Running Wild*, where she played the daughter of Ray Brooks' lead character for two series in 1987-89.

Making BBC play *Pressures* in 1988 she was spotted by *EastEnders* producer Julia Smith, who auditioned her for the part of Cindy, a girl working on a hat stall and intended as love interest for Simon Wicks (Nick Berry) for just 11 episodes. The fiesty and selfish Cindy soon became embroiled in various love triangles, ending up engaged to Ian Beale by 1990. After their dramatic break-up, Cindy left the series (Collins branching out by presenting Channel 4's controversial youth show *The Word*), but returned in 1992. After cheating on Ian with David Wicks, creating a custody battle, Cindy had a drive-by hitman shoot Ian.

The *grand guignol* storyline made Collins a small-screen star and when she exited *EastEnders* in 1996 there were any number of TV vehicles built around her: the female ensemble piece *Real Women* (1998-9) was a well-received hit; the much-hyped, frothy holiday rep melodrama *Sunburn* (1999-2000) perhaps less so (although Collins made number 28 in the pop charts with her theme single). She also took the female lead in three series of picturesque comedy drama *Two Thousand Acres of Sky* (2001-3).

The *Illustrated Mum*, a film made for Channel 4 in 2003, based on Jacqueline Wilson's novel, saw Collins play a tattooed, depressive single mother and the unglamorous role was one of her most critically acclaimed performances. It was informed by Collins' own personal battles with depression and anorexia.

Collins made a foray into supernatural fantasy in 2004 with two episodes of *Sea of Souls* and although she only appeared in the second story, her photograph launched the series with a *Radio Times* front cover, marking her star status.

For her *Doctor Who* role of McDonnell the usually glamorous actress was not allowed to wear make-up and spent days with grease in her hair, covered in baby oil 'sweat'. Of the part she said; "She's a woman in a man's world. She's quite sassy but also passionate about her crew. She's strong but not a feminist type."

Despite her huge variety of roles, viewers still wanted to see Collins back as a soap queen. Cindy Beale was long dead (killed off-screen in 1998) but in 2011 former *Doctor Who* producer Phil Collinson, now producing *Coronation Street*, helped Collins settle into Weatherfield where she played Stella Price, the new landlady of the Rovers Return and estranged secret mother of Leanne Battersby, until 2014. ■

Index

Page numbers in *italic* type refer to pictures.

M

N

O

P

R

S